# Financial Promise
# for the Poor

# Financial Promise
# for the Poor

## How Groups Build Microsavings

Edited by

KIM WILSON, MALCOLM HARPER,
AND MATTHEW GRIFFITH

Kumarian Press
*An Imprint of Stylus Publishing*

*Financial Promise for the Poor: How Groups Build Microsavings*
Published in 2010 in the United States of America by Kumarian Press,
22883 Quicksilver Drive, Sterling, VA 20166 USA.

The text of this book is set in 11/13 Garamond.
Editing and book design by Joan Weber Laflamme.
Proofread by Beth Richards.
Index by Robert Swanson.

⊚ The paper used in this publication meets the minimum requirements of the American National Standard for Information Sciences—
 Permanence of Paper for printed Library Materials, ANSI Z39.48–1984.

---

**Library of Congress Cataloging-in-Publication Data**

Financial promise for the poor : how groups build microsavings /
edited by Kim Wilson, Malcolm Harper, and Matthew Griffith.
   p. cm.
  Includes bibliographical references and index.
  ISBN 978–1–56549–339–1 (pbk. : alk. paper) — ISBN 978–1–56549–
340–7 (cloth : alk. paper)
1. Microfinance—Developing countries. 2. Savings and loan associations—Developing countries. 3. Rotating credit associations—Developing countries. 4. Poor—Developing countries. I. Wilson, Kim.
II. Harper, Malcolm, 1935– III. Griffith, Matthew.
  HG178.33.F56 2010
  332.1'752—dc22

                                                            2010011068

# Contents

**PART 3**
**MORE WAYS OF SKINNING THE CAT,**
**AND DIFFERENT KINDS OF CATS**

# Illustrations

*Opening Photos*

**Introduction.** Malian women carry savings, gleaned from working the fields, to a group meeting at a village nearby.

**1.** Charles Oranje, president of the Gatwichera Railway Savings Club, Kibera, Kenya, seeks members who fled during election violence.

**5.** Despite the Haitian earthquake of 2010, which devastated the financial activities of much of Port-Au-Prince, Brave Warriors, a savings group of twenty members, continues to meet every Thursday evening.

**9.** Malian group leaders track deposits and loan payments in full view of group membership.

**15.** Savings group member in Bamyan Province, Afghanistan, contributes monthly savings to the designated group accountants.

**18.** Doris Dvube, a savings-group member in Nzameya, Swaziland, explains her personal savings-and-lending plan to fellow group members.

**Conclusion.** Three generations of savers in Rajasthan, India, invest their savings and loans in water harvesting and school tuition.

# Acronyms

| | |
|---|---|
| AKRSP | Aga Khan Rural Support Programme (Pakistan) |
| ASCA | accumulating savings-and-credit association |
| BARA | Bureau for Applied Research in Anthropology |
| BRK | Rural Development Bank |
| CCR | Asociación de Comunidades para Desarrollo de Chalatenango (El Salvador) |
| CEDAC | Cambodian Center for Study and Development in Agriculture |
| CLP | Chars Livelihood Project (Northern Bangladesh) |
| CMLF | community-managed loan fund |
| CRS | Catholic Relief Services |
| DCCH | Development Comunitaire Chretien Haitien |
| FSDK | Kenya Financial Sector Deepening Trust |
| HDFC | Housing Development Finance Corporation (India) |
| IIED | International Institute for Environment and Development |
| LPD | Lembaga Perkreditan Desa (village-led financial institutions) |
| MFI | microfinance institution |
| MuSos | Mutuelles de solidarite |
| NABARD | National Bank for Agriculture and Rural Development (India) |

| | |
|---|---|
| NCAER | National Council of Applied Economic Research (India) |
| NGO | nongovernmental organization |
| RBI | Reserve Bank of India |
| ROSCA | rotating savings-and-credit association |
| SfC | Saving for Change |
| SHG | self-help group |
| SILC | Savings and Internal Lending Communities |
| USAID | United States Agency for International Development |
| VSLA | Village Savings and Loan Associations |

# Financial Promise
for the Poor

Malian women carry savings,
gleaned from working the fields,
to a group meeting at a village nearby.

# Introduction

Hot money, hat money, box money—each means money saved in the fellowship of others, usually just a few others, in what this book calls a savings group. These groups are a kind of club in which people come together for the purposes of saving and borrowing. Groups can include men and women, but the majority of savings group members across the world are women.

In southern Haiti, for example, ten women might join together weekly to place the equivalent of a dollar per member into a group fund. Each week one member will carry the full purse home, to spend as she chooses. Members will meet week in and week out, always making their one-dollar contributions as they do, and will continue to meet until each has received the ten-dollar purse. Once this cycle is complete, members may decide to start saving anew.

The cash that a group collects helps a member pay for a trip to the city, rent a truck to haul the harvest, buy textbooks, or purchase a gift. Each woman could have saved the money on her own, arriving at the same goal of ten dollars in ten weeks, and she could have done so without the company of others. Had she chosen to save by herself, however, she would have risked her ten dollars never materializing. She knows it would be unlikely that any coins trickling into her household would coalesce into the desired dollars, and that it would be far more likely that a persuasive husband or plaintive child would announce better uses for her idle change: the purchase of a cool drink or a piece of candy, for example. She herself might be tempted to spend loose cash at the local lottery. The money would vanish bit by bit, almost imperceptibly.

Saving alone, a woman is obligated to no one. Saving with others, she is obligated to her group. She owes them the courtesy of her dollar when it is due. This kind of group, in which

1

members take turns receiving the lump sum, is called a rotating savings and credit association, or ROSCA, an ungainly term but one widely used in the development community, and so we shall use it here. ROSCAs finance the payment of rents and school fees, new refrigerators, cars, pots and pans, clothes, tombstones, weddings, and woven blankets. The core structures of the ROSCA in countries like Japan (where it is known as *Kou*), Ethiopia *(Iqub)*, and Mexico *(Tanda)* are identical. In Harvard Square, ROSCAs made up of taxi drivers function in exactly the same way. Each week, many drivers place money with one driver, called the banker, and each week one driver walks away with the whole sum. Known by different names in different cultures, ROSCAs tick with the precision of a Swiss clock. They run on discipline, commitment, honor, shame, thrift, tradition, and trust.

There is another kind of savings group called an accumulating savings and credit association (ASCA). ASCAs are similar to ROSCAs in many ways. Like a ROSCA, an ASCA relies on the regular deposits of its members. Unlike a ROSCA, an ASCA holds onto its savings. No single person walks away with the fund each round. The money pools over the course of months or even years. Regular contributions come into the fund as savings deposits and flow out of the fund as loans. Every so often, perhaps once a year, members of the ASCA might choose to dissolve the fund, distributing its contents back to members. A distribution would include a member's savings plus her share of any income that had come into the fund during the year, such as interest on loans, fees and fines, or money from group income-producing activities.

ROSCAs are already well documented, and so this book focuses on ASCAs.[1] Many people in poor parts of the world use both ASCAs and ROSCAs as part of their larger folk-banking strategy. Some ASCAs adopt a ROSCA feature whereby a portion of the money stays in the fund and a portion rotates among members. And some ROSCAs adopt an ASCA feature whereby the group begins to accumulate a portion of deposited funds, using it to make loans to members. The services of folk banking function as smoothly on the shores of the Nile as they do in the hills of Darjeeling or the slums of Nairobi.

## Why Groups and Not Microfinance Institutions?

Why would members choose to save in a group rather than saving in a microfinance institution (MFI)?

First, savings groups are themselves miniature, unregulated banks where savers save and borrowers borrow. One could say that savings groups *are* MFIs, albeit small ones.

Second, many microfinance institutions do not offer savings services. Convenient, reliable deposit services with banks or MFIs may be available to some, but they remain out of reach for most of the world's poor. Even where deposit services are available, many savers choose to save in their groups as well. They like the discipline of making regular deposits, something usually not required by formal financial providers, and they like the convenience of saving close to home.

Third, groups may give members better loan services than those offered at the local microfinance institution. The products of MFIs are often rigid. For example, a borrower might need a six-month loan to be repaid at the end of the term, but the local MFI might offer a four-month loan to be repaid monthly. By using her group, a member can shape a loan suited to her needs and capacity to repay. Moreover, an MFI is likely to issue loans strictly for small-business use. A borrower, especially a poor borrower, may not want to finance a business; it would be too risky. Instead, she might prefer to use the loan to repair a bicycle, to pay a midwife, or to contribute to a funeral. The savings group would be more likely than an MFI to finance these expenses.

Fourth, when a borrower takes a loan from an MFI, the interest charged, which can be as high as 2 percent, 5 percent, or even 10 percent per month, travels out of the hands of the borrower and into the hands of the MFI. In contrast, if she borrows from her group, the interest accrues to the fund and therefore to all its members, including her. Members enjoy interest income from loans as a return on their savings.

To savers, the money deposited into the communal chest, bowl, or bag is hard-won and precious, and they do not want to lose it. Members work too hard to stockpile what little change comes their way to let it dissipate. To borrowers, the money from the group is a life-support system—it can fund medical expenses just as easily as the purchase of grain to trade—and therefore borrowers are just as reluctant as savers to let their funds fritter away. And while members may also use banks and MFIs, they often see their groups as valuable and worth protecting, more personal in their feel and immediate in their services, more reliable, and more convenient than the formal institutions.

## The Savings of Groups

Savers in groups prefer to save in the company of others. They like the habit, the practice, and the pledge of saving regularly, even when their incomes arrive in fits and starts. Sometimes members want a reason to gather, just to see one another, and saving in a group justifies a gathering. Many women, especially rural women, have an interest in leaving the doorstep of the home or the dirt of the field in search of other women—with a good excuse in hand. Life can be lonely without that excuse, and meeting to manage money often satisfies even the most inquisitive of husbands and mothers-in-law.

Group members find ingenious ways to save, even when saving is difficult. Through small acts of thrift members are able to collect a few coins during the week. Those coins transform into regular savings deposits made at group meetings. How do members come by this money? Some cut back on tea, or sweets, or tobacco. Some sell a chicken or a few eggs, or put aside a handful of rice each day and then, later in the week, before the meeting, turn the chicken or rice into cash.

A long delay can stand between the cash designated for savings and the actual moment of saving: the deposit made into the common fund at the group meeting. What do members do as they wait for deposit day to approach? Some hide cash from family members by stitching coins into their clothes, stuffing them into bamboo rafters, burying them in the ground, lending them to a neighbor, or giving them to a trusted group member to hold until deposit day. In countries like Kenya, where mobile telephone banking services are available, members can store for deposit day by adding value to their mobile accounts.

## The Loans of Groups

Members use loans according to carefully crafted group rules. Some groups are flexible and allow members to borrow for any reason. For example, members might use a loan to a buy a dress or supplies, or to fix a roof or a broken cart. When incomes dip and members lack cash for basic needs, groups might grant loans to members to buy food or fuel. Other groups are far more prescriptive and ask members to borrow for certain purposes: the purchase of raw silk to weave into cloth, musical instruments to strengthen the local singing troupe, or livestock to fatten and sell. Some groups agree that at harvest time, when the local grain market is flooded, members may borrow and even should borrow to finance household necessities. In this way members can hold on to their crops, riding out a period of low market prices and then selling when prices rise.

The interest charged by groups to their members varies. Groups may reject charging any interest at all, as in areas that observe Islamic law. However, most groups the editors of this book have visited do charge interest. Some groups charge low interest on loans, such as 2 percent per month, believing that the poorest members are the most likely to need a loan, yet are least likely to have the capacity to pay high interest rates. These groups might decide that wealthier members should not gain from those facing hard times and keep rates low. Other groups and other members feel quite different. They believe that the prospect of a healthy return on savings was central to their decision to join, and that their savings had better yield a good rate, say 10 percent per month, or else they will leave the group and invest elsewhere.

Variation does not stop at interest rates. Young groups, still building their capital and developing a reliable culture of lending and repayment, often set limits on loan maturity. One-month, three-month, and six-month loan paybacks are common, with interest due weekly or monthly and the full principal paid at the end of the term. In more mature groups, which have greater sums available and a membership of "veteran bankers," loan maturities may stretch beyond a year, especially when a loan is used for the purchase of land or larger livestock.

## The Size of Groups and Decision Making

Savings groups differ in size. Some include a handful of members who reside in the same village. Others, operating in more densely populated areas, have dozens of members who hale from the same neighborhood or work in the same marketplace. Smaller groups might meld into larger ones. For example, in Sri Lanka three groups of about fifteen members decided to merge into a group of forty-five. They calculated that members would have a chance at larger loans if the communal fund had more savers depositing into it. A larger fund would accommodate larger loans. The opposite is also true. Groups may find their membership size unwieldy and choose to divide themselves into smaller groups. This practice is especially common in places like India, where groups can grow quickly in size. Still others, for instance in Nicaragua, want to keep their groups small but will meet in a cluster to hold a raffle or discuss social issues.

Groups with fewer than ten members usually make decisions jointly, including decisions about which members may receive a loan. Larger groups often elect a committee that decides loan priorities and manages the cash. The committee, in the presence of all members, collects savings deposits and loan payments. It might include a treasurer to manage the cash box, a counter to count the money as it comes in and goes out, a recorder to keep cash records, and a group leader to preside over meetings.

Members themselves decide the amount each member saves, how often members make deposits, the repayment period of loans, the frequency of loan payments, interest on loans, and fines for late savings deposits or late loan payments. For example, a group may decide that members should save one dollar per month every month, and make that deposit at a regular monthly meeting. Another might decide on the same one dollar amount, but deposited every two weeks. Still another may set flexible savings rules ("save when you can") while enforcing strict loan repayment rules ("repay your full loan within three months"); or the reverse ("save on time but repay when you can").

Members decide who makes the lending decisions within the group, when to hold meetings, and the penalties for nonattendance. They also decide who can be a member. Some groups allow only people who live or work nearby to join. Others insist members be married to join, and others that members be unmarried. Groups might include members with the same skills, such as weaving or stitching, or different skills to keep the group diverse and members uncompetitive. Some want their members to have similar incomes so that choosing a savings rate is easy. Others want to make sure their group has a good mix of "net borrowers," people who borrow more than they save, and "net savers," people who save more than they borrow. Sometimes groups lend outside the group, often charging outsiders a higher rate of interest than that charged to members.

Groups vary widely on when and how a member may withdraw her savings. Some allow members to leave only at a predetermined time, such as when loans are collected, the fund is full, and its monies can be distributed to every member. Still others allow the departure of a member and keep a cash balance for just such an occasion. Others still have no such provision, and conflict may ensue as members work out how they will return savings to a departing member or if they will return her savings at all.

## Depth and Multiple Memberships

Belonging to one group is a good start, but for some, membership in one group does not provide enough financial diversity to meet household needs. One study shows that the average household in one village has membership in seven different savings groups.[2]

There are several advantages to belonging to many groups. A member has multiple sources from which to borrow and need not depend on a single source or single group for all her needs. Since different groups are likely to have different savings requirements, the saver can balance her various memberships according to her own cash flow. She can save in several places, hedging her risk that one group will lose her funds.

## Kinds of Savings Groups

*Customary savings groups* are groups formed in the wild, as it were, without the oversight of an NGO (nongovernmental organization) or any other institution; they spring from tradition or the experience of neighbors. Members convene meetings on their own, receiving guidance from friends, family, schoolteachers, religious leaders, or peers. Customary groups can be natural extensions of other kinds of informal clubs,[3] where people already come together to clear land, build homes, fell trees, produce soap, repair fishing nets, or harvest crops. These new financial groups may grow from handicraft cooperatives, sports clubs, or parents' associations.

*Promoted savings groups* are groups promoted by someone or some agency that usually is not a member of the group. Promoted groups are like customary groups with one exception: an organization—the national government, a local NGO or charity, or an international agency—actually forms the groups. The promoting organization sends in volunteers or pays trainers to form new groups, usually ASCAs. In some instances a government, bank, or nonprofit organization may pay promoters to form or support groups. In other instances members will pay promoters directly for their services. And many times, promoters go unpaid, finding their time well spent in helping friends and neighbors. Some volunteers have started dozens of groups and find reward in the social and economic progress of people in their care.

An organization will promote groups for several reasons. First, it may believe that savings groups are a good place for households to store money. Adults may not have access to bank accounts, especially in poor areas. They need a cushion of funds to protect them against emergencies, or a place in which to save or from which to borrow for family survival, well-being, or improvement.

Second, promoting organizations may believe that membership in a group helps individuals develop confidence. Members report that being part of a group gives them the chance to increase their cash as well as their household status. Women members begin to feel important, and this importance boosts their self-respect. After joining a group and feeling the accomplishment of saving or repaying a loan, members feel motivated to take on other challenges. They sit on school committees, join community task forces, collectively cultivate land, build roads, or run for local political office.

Third, promoting organizations may find savings groups to be a springboard for other kinds of support. For example, consider an organization that wants to bring health services to a village. If women already meet for regular savings and loan activities, they might be willing to attend a workshop on hygiene or prenatal care. They might borrow from their fund to finance a midwife or to purchase mosquito nets. Consider an organization that specializes in rural technologies: bio-gas production; rainwater harvesting; solar lighting. Savings groups are a perfect platform for these organizations to introduce new technologies. Training groups costs less than training individuals, and groups may collectively take on and even finance the additional services.

Depending on where you stand on the globe (and possibly which model you have chosen to champion), you will encounter different names for promoted savings groups: self-help groups (SHGs), Mutuelles de solidarite (MuSos), or more broadly, community-managed loan funds (CMLFs).[4]

Several brand names are used to describe ASCAs. CARE calls the groups it promotes VSLAs (Village Savings and Loan Associations), Catholic Relief Services in Africa calls its groups SILCs (Savings and Internal Lending Communities), and Oxfam America calls its groups SfC (Saving for Change) groups. Their basic idea is the same; they all help form groups that follow the ASCA model.

## Scale and Expansion

How do groups multiply? More to the point, how do promoting organizations expand the number of groups throughout a geographic region?

Promoting organizations increase group numbers in several ways. They retain virtual armies of staff whose job it is to form groups. They also organize village or neighborhood volunteers— including members of existing groups—to take up the task of forming groups. They train local entrepreneurs to develop groups, and then those entrepreneurs, paid by the groups themselves, keep creating and supporting groups. Some organizations combine these expansion strategies and approaches like promoter certification and area franchises to build their programs.

## Quality and Sustainability

What makes a savings group a savings group? And how long must members stay grouped to produce impact or to be considered a "good" group?

Answers differ. Some organizations believe groups should persist over time and feel a sense of failure when groups split apart. For example, many organizations in India insist that self-help groups, as savings groups there are called, work best and offer members lasting benefits only when groups remain intact for many years, with their original membership still active.

In contrast, other promoting organizations believe that groups can form and dissolve without compromising their purpose or any gains made by members. These organizations reason that members will retain the discipline and the financial rewards of good savings practices. For example, the VSLA model automatically limits the duration of groups' financial life. Groups collect all outstanding loans and interest, distribute savings, and start afresh at least once a year. No one minds that the group reorganizes, even with new members entering and seasoned ones departing. Once the group reconstitutes, it can continue the activities of saving, borrowing, and cashing out from time to time.

Which attitude or belief is correct? Probably both, maybe neither. Promoting organizations tend to fall into doctrinal camps, with one camp declaring that groups must be time bound and another declaring that groups should last indefinitely. These camps seem silly because members themselves should make important decisions about the duration of a group. The editors believe that dissolving a fund early in a group's development is probably a good idea so that dissatisfied members may leave without undue disruption. But to insist or even suggest that groups follow a specific formula is folly, equivalent to a paint-by-the-numbers approach to community finance, disregarding and disrespecting local custom and decision making.

## What Is Wrong with Groups?

There is nothing wrong with groups as such; however, some groups have been known to mishandle the money of their savers, steal funds from illiterate members, and channel loans to group leaders. Less deliberately, groups have simply lost the money of members or allowed funds from the cash box to dwindle through poor record-keeping.

Groups form, disperse, and form again. Yet, by themselves, groups do not and cannot heal all wounds. Financial poverty requires solutions on many fronts. Banks and MFIs must offer better savings services to complement the savings of groups. Members need and want regulated, formal, even insured, savings accounts, both as groups and as individuals within groups. They would like the confidentiality that goes with individual accounts. They also want individual credit and insurance. While groups are a good start, they remain only part of a financial whole.

## The Organization of This Book

This book is organized into five parts, each reflecting a theme of savings groups, with the main emphasis being on savings groups that accumulate funds over time.

Part 1, *Do-It-Yourself Finance*, focuses on self-started customary savings groups. This collection of articles describes groups that have formed without encouragement or funding from banks, governments, or NGOs. Members have taken their inspiration from savings practices already in the community, from entrepreneurs who make their livings managing groups, or from local religious and social custom. The groups profiled range from simple ROSCAs to sophisticated groups that have ingeniously molded the basic ASCA into financial hubs of surprisingly versatility.

Part 2, *Now They Need Us (Or Do They?)*, addresses how NGOs, banks, and governments help groups to form and become strong over time. With the help of outside expertise, groups act as provisional banks, offering members a safe place to store their savings, borrow at flexible and friendly terms, and earn interest, in most cases, on their savings. These groups often distribute their funds to the members, clearing their fund to a zero balance once a year. Members usually start saving, borrowing, and earning interest anew in the next year. International agencies have learned many tips to share with groups on meeting procedures, savings and loan rules, membership selection, and record-keeping.

Part 3, *More Ways of Skinning the Cat, and Different Kinds of Cats*, shows how some individuals and agencies that promote savings groups have adapted the core ideas and methods presented in Part 2 to meet challenges on the ground, suit needs or practices of group members, or satisfy a quest for group sustainability. Authors explore ways to help groups become strong, proliferate throughout an area, and reach a very poor membership in need of services. Examples show how organizations have harnessed the power of the market, volunteerism, information technology, banking, and conditional aid (subsidy with a few strings attached) to improve and expand financial self-service.

Part 4, *Sinking, Swimming, and Staying Afloat*, describes the internal evaluation efforts of agencies that fund the formation of savings groups. International foundations and governments are fueling the growth of the savings sector with unprecedented amounts of money. Tens of millions of dollars are being poured into this new industry. Do groups work, and are they worth the money that is being paid for their development? These chapters examine early efforts to review the performance of savings groups and the aid agencies and local organizations that promote them. Together, the articles reflect on the durability of groups, their effect on local financial service, and their potential impact on the lives of group members and their families.

Part 5, *An Alternative, or Something Altogether Different?,* offers four views on the savings-group industry. These articles attempt to answer the question of whether groups might be formed more efficiently, linked more successfully to additional financial services (indeed, whether they ought to become linked at all), and what their function is and might be, beyond savings and lending.

## Notes

[1] For a more thorough treatment of ROSCAs, see *Money-Go-Rounds: The Importance of Rotating Savings and Credit Associations for Women,* ed. Shirley Ardener and Sandra Burman (Oxford, UK: Berg, 1996).

[2] Abhijit Sharma and Brett Matthews, "On an Informal Frontier: The ASCAs of Lower Assam," in *Life Savings: How the Poor Use Groups to Pool Money and Hedge Risk*, ed. Kim Wilson, Malcolm Harper, and Matthew Griffith (Bloomfield, CT: Kumarian Press, 2009), 43–56.

[3] Hans Dieter Seibel, "Traditional Cooperatives among the Kpelle in Liberia," in *Africana Collecta*, ed. Dieter Oberndoerfer (Guetersloh: Bertelsmann Universitaetsverlag, 1968), 115–25.

[4] Jennifer Isern, L. B. Prakash, Anuradha Pillai, Syed Hashemi, Robert Peck Christen, Gautam J. Ivatury, Richard Rosenberg, "Sustainability of Self-Help Groups in India: Two Analyses," CGAP Occasional Paper 12 (2007).

Charles Oranje, president of the Gatwichera Railway Savings
Club, Kibera, Kenya, seeks members who fled
during election violence.

# PART I

# DO-IT-YOURSELF FINANCE

This book is not mainly about customary or self-formed groups. It is about groups that have been promoted by us, the writers, the outsiders. We must not forget, however, that the vast majority of savings groups owe nothing to "us"; they have been formed and are managed by their members, without the benefit (if it is a benefit; we must never assume that it is) of outside advice or assistance.

Simple ROSCAs are probably almost as old as society itself. A contemporary account refers to such groups in Japan eight hundred years ago, and some two hundred different names have been identified that are used to describe these groups.[1] Many of these names are derived from *tontine*, a French word that was apparently first used in the seventeenth century, based on the practices of an Italian banker named Francisco Tonti. Others are based on the West African term *susu*, or the Arabic *komiti*. Most of the names, however, are local.

Customary savings groups are almost universal. Money is not their sole medium of exchange; some groups use bricks, or rice, or labor, or just about any homogeneous commodity to which all the members have access. Nor do they depend on written records; simple memory is enough.

Most of the promoted groups described in this book are ASCAs. Here, members' contributions are not all paid out at every meeting, as they are in a classic ROSCA. Funds may be kept for a time when several members want money; or lent out at a profit, to members or sometimes to non-members; or the funds may be used to buy a common asset. Many natural, customary groups also have such refinements, however. Sophistication is not exclusive to promoted groups.

This first part is about customary groups. We have included these accounts in order to remind ourselves that "our" promoted groups are not necessarily the best. Also, it is important to acknowledge that promoters can do little more than learn from what people have been doing for centuries, and then use their learning to make some modest improvements to traditional systems, and to spread the word more widely.

Jahns's paper describes a women's group in Kenya and a men's group in Tanzania. Both are strong and resilient. Both include a number of unique features, like the use of music. And neither owes anything to external advice. The members have developed their own systems, based on what they have seen their neighbors doing. It is difficult to see how an external adviser could make any improvements to either of them.

The *Xonchoi xamitis* of Assam, described by Sharma and Matthews, are similarly successful. Over 70 percent of households in a particular part of Assam are said to be members of them, and many households belong to as many as seven or even more of these groups.

Pradhan describes a *dhukuti*, or savings group, in central Nepal, started by her mother. It has grown into a cooperative with over half a million dollars in capital. Again, the entire venture was based on local knowledge, with no donor or other external assistance, a surprising feat in a sadly over-aided country.

Our last genuinely natural case is that of the village savings and credit institutions of Bali, based on the strong local traditions of thrift and duty, but officially recognized by the provincial government in 1984. The original groups were totally customary in their origins and operations, and the government's role was only to recognize and regularize them, not to promote them.

These groups are all very different, and they are only a tiny sample of the myriad variants of customary groups that are to be found worldwide, in better-off as well as poor communities. They do however have one thing in common; "we" can learn from all of them.

# Chapter 1

# Teacups and Hand Hoes

*Home-Grown Savings Groups in East Africa*

ELKE JAHNS

## The Merry-go-round

*We are crowded in Betty's living room. The dung floor has been carefully swept, the chairs neatly covered with homemade doilies. Alone or in groups of two or three, women in bright head scarves and khangas enter with cheerful greetings. They each hand Betty a new green-rimmed teacup as she welcomes them into her home.*

Betty has invited me to attend her women's group meeting on her farm near the village of Kabula in western Kenya. "We just do a simple merry-go-round," Betty explains. "We each put some money in the basket, and a different person gets the whole amount each time, to use as she likes." But after a little probing, it turns out this group is much more than a simple merry-go-round; it is also a farming cooperative, savings bank, insurance provider, prayer group, and support network.

Betty and her neighbors formed this group over ten years ago, on their own initiative, based on a typical merry-go-round format. Their group comprises fifteen women, and they meet on the fifteenth and thirtieth of each month. Attendance is mandatory, though members can send a daughter or sister in their place in case of other unavoidable commitments. Every meeting opens with a prayer and closes with a song.

Each cycle of the merry-go-round starts with a lottery; members draw slips of paper to determine when they will get their turn to host the meeting and keep the collection basket. During the first few years, members each contributed 100 Kenyan shillings (about $1.30) to the basket at every meeting. The group recently decided to raise each person's contribution to $6.50 per meeting.

So far, Betty's group sounds like a classic rotating savings and credit association (ROSCA). Stuart Rutherford has called the ROSCA "the world's most efficient and cheapest financial intermediary device."[2] ROSCAs require no elaborate record keeping, no safe places for storing group savings, no outside intervention, no indebtedness. Because they are so easy to form and manage, tens of thousands of ROSCAs have been active on every continent for many years. They are known by a variety of local names: merry-go-rounds in East Africa, self-help groups in India, and *mutuelles* in Haiti, among many others.

## Beyond the Merry-go-round: Group Savings and Insurance

Betty's group started out as a simple ROSCA. However, unconstrained by external expectations or models, Betty and her friends added various features to their group over time, crafting them into a unique recipe for financial success.

Moving beyond their basic merry-go-round, the women added a group fund that acts as a longer-term savings account or insurance fund. At every group meeting, after depositing the $6.50 into the basket, members also contribute $0.65 each into a group savings fund managed by the treasurer. In case of death or serious illness in a member's family, the group can vote to contribute money to the family from the special fund. Any money remaining in the fund at the end of the year is redistributed evenly among all members. These additions, bringing with them more complicated procedures and services, make Betty's group an accumulating savings and credit association (ASCA), in the parlance of academics and practitioners.

## Beyond the ASCA: Farming, Funerals, and Teacups

Betty's group is much more than a mechanism for saving and transferring money. In some ways it also resembles a mini-farming cooperative. If one group member has a plot of land that she is not using, the women all farm it together and the profits are divided among the group members at the end of the year.

And then there are the teacups. Before each meeting the upcoming hostess may request small household items that she needs—cups or plates, for instance. Everyone then shows up at the next meeting with, say, a green-rimmed teacup from the second stall in the market. At the end of the meeting, the hostess has a brand new set of fifteen matching teacups, a tangible symbol of her group's solidarity. If she really does not need teacups, or would rather save up for a bigger purchase (a few chickens, a goat, a sheet of corrugated iron to fix the roof) she can request a little extra money instead.

Perhaps most important, this group provides a reliable support network for women who continually face hardship and uncertainty. This solidarity aspect of the group is so ingrained that Betty does not even think to include their actions of mutual support in her initial list of group activities. "If someone in the group has a funeral for a family member, we all attend as a group, and we help buy and prepare food together as a group," Betty explains. "Or if someone has a wedding or has visitors, we go and help out with the preparations. Or if one of us is sick, we take turns visiting her in the hospital."

## Dancing Farmers

*It is twilight in the village of Mahaha, in the Lake Zone of Tanzania. We are standing in a dusty vacant lot, milling among Henry's neighbors—mostly farmers and schoolchildren. Suddenly a twangy wail sings out from the crowd. A man is playing a kadete—an instrument made of a large hollow gourd and a few strings of sisal fibers, played by stretching the strings and bowing across them. The tune is repetitive, dance-like, and mournful; it is fiddle and banjo, Japanese flute and Gregorian chant all in one.*

*We see that the children have moved aside, and the farmers have broken into even lines, four rows of four. Blasts from two silver whistles start the men moving in time to the music. Their dark muscular arms swing their hand hoes; their bare feet stamp on the packed dirt. They step to the sides, forward and back, swinging the hoes from hand to hand and high over their heads. It is an intricate dance, perfectly choreographed. Step step STAMP, swing, turn, step step swing, THWACK—sixteen hand hoes hit the ground in unison—step step STAMP, swing, turn, step step swing, THWACK.*

## More Than Just a Song and Dance

Afterward, Henry tells us a bit more about these farmers. There are several such groups in Mahaha, he says; three use *kadetes*, others use drums. This arrangement of music and dance is how they plow their fields, from eight in the morning to five in the afternoon, in the hot sun, with short breaks for porridge and lunch. They bring their whistles and *kadete* with them. Their neat lines of dance will become deep furrows between rows of maize and beans and cotton. *Step step STAMP, swing THWACK.* To the rhythm of their music, all day, every day of the planting season, they till the soil, visiting in turn the small vegetable gardens of each group member. Like a New England barn-raising, this is part of a social support system that has been practiced by the Sukuma people for generations. After preparing their own fields, they branch out to the fields of elderly or sick neighbors who cannot plow for themselves. In return, they get a meal and a small contribution to ensure they can keep their hand hoes in good repair

Frank Gunderson, an ethnomusicologist, has studied these Sukuma musician farmer groups. The groups emerged among local cotton farmers during the British colonial era, developing out of existing musical traditions related to medicinal societies, hunting groups, porters, and military organizations.[3] Gunderson is particularly intrigued by the social support networks these groups create:

Music performance such as this not only lightens the work load and transforms work into something more playful, but also performs a role in creating a dynamic and heightened group consciousness, creating an environment where everyday village discourse and political commentary are encouraged, enjoyed, and reflected upon. Working together with music becomes more than simply a technical means of accomplishing agricultural tasks; it plays a crucial role in establishing closeness, mutual support, and community solidarity.[4]

Hans Dieter Seibel describes similar groups on the other side of the continent:

> In March 1967, on one of my first field trips in Liberia, I had the opportunity to observe a group of a dozen Mano peasants cutting trees in a field belonging to one of them. Before they started their work, they placed hoe-shaped masks in a small circle, chanted words and—turned into animals. One turned into a lion, another one into a bush hog, and so on, and they continued to imitate those animals throughout the whole day, as they worked hard on their land. . . . I learned that they worked as a group, tackling the fields of each one in turn.[5]

Such groups are only a small fraction of the many types of savings groups Seibel has described around the world. From West Africa, Yoruba slaves carried the tradition of rotating savings to the Caribbean in the sixteenth century, where it is still practiced today. Seibel cites similar groups in Ethiopia, Egypt, Indonesia, the Philippines, and Guatemala.[6] Each group has evolved its own unique characteristics, reflecting the local culture and values and needs of its members.

## Conclusion

Parker Shipton was struck by the diversity, strength, and prevalence of traditional savings groups, and he called on development practitioners to consider existing savings and credit mechanisms before imposing their own models. Group ownership is key, he said, when describing the *osusus*, Gambian

ROSCAs. Though outsiders may be able to help spread ideas, "part of the appeal of the *osusu* to its members is that it is truly their own. *Osusu* groups are functioning comparatively well . . . and in the end the best way of helping them might be to leave them alone."[7]

Betty's group in Kenya and the dancing farmers in Tanzania are but two examples of the rich variety of savings groups that have sprung up in poor communities around the world. The teacups, the hand hoes, the *kadete*, and the merry-go-round are just some of the many means that people have found to help themselves and one another, building on their own traditions and ideas to create groups that match their needs, groups that they can call their own.

## Notes

[1] F. A. J. Bouman, "ROSCA: On the Origin of the Species," *Savings and Development* 19, no. 2 (1995): 117–48.

[2] Stuart Rutherford, *The Poor and Their Money: An Essay about Financial Services for Poor People* (New Delhi, India: Oxford University Press, 2000), 22.

[3] Frank Gunderson, "From 'Dancing with Porcupines' to 'Twirling a Hoe': Musical Labor Transformed in Sukumaland, Tanzania," *Africa Today* 48, no. 4 (winter 2001): 3.

[4] Ibid., 4.

[5] Hans Dieter Seibel, "Rural Finance: Mainstreaming Informal Financial Institutions," *Journal of Developmental Entrepreneurship* 6, no. 1 (2001): 83–84.

[6] Ibid.

[7] Parker Shipton, *How Gambians Save—and What Their Strategies Imply for International Aid* (Washington DC: World Bank, 1990).

## Chapter 2

# *Dhukuti*—A Real Treasure

## *The Growth of a Savings Group Idea in Nepal*

### Shailee Pradhan

### Introduction

Planted on a fertile hill, the small Nepalese town of Bandipur once hosted a vibrant economy. In the 1800s and early 1900s Bandipur was a commercial center along the India-Tibet trade route. However, after a sweeping political and administrative reorganization in the early 1960s—including the construction of a modern highway that bypassed Bandipur completely— regional economic activity shifted to the towns of Dumre and Damauli, which enjoyed better access to the markets of Kathmandu. The once thriving economic center turned into all but a ghost town.

My parents were one of the families that left Bandipur for Kathmandu as a result of the economic decline. During this transition phase, increasingly scattered Bandipures were able to keep their social ties alive through the initiative of Chiz Kumar Shrestha, now a household name in the region. In 1993, Shrestha founded the Bandipur Social Development Committee in an effort to preserve and promote the cultural and historical heritage of Bandipur. Central among the committee's activities were support for local enterprises and an effort to bring sustainable prosperity to the people of Bandipur.

A few years after its founding, the female members of the committee established a women's development subcommittee. Fifty women invested five thousand rupees each, about $67 per member, with the understanding that the investment would earn 10 percent annual interest and be returned to them in five years. The Bandipur Women's Development Sub-Committee was born, starting with $3,500 in capital.

Once established, the subcommittee faced an even more challenging task: what to do with its investment. The group wanted something that would bring about both social and financial improvement, something that allowed Bandipur women to remain connected and productive. But its options were limited, both because the group was run by volunteers and because of the small size of the investment, which put constraints on what kind of business ventures the group could fund. Moreover, the group had promised to give a good financial return to its members, which further curtailed its choice of investment.

## From a Storage Box to Informal Finance

My mother, a member of the women's group, had heard of ROSCAs, popularly known as *dhukuti* in Nepal. The evolution of *dhukuti* goes back to an age-old institution, the *dhikur* (literally, a storage box for valuables or food grains), which the ethnic Thakali developed centuries ago in the course of the trans-Himalayan trade.[1] The *dhukuti*'s first form was probably that of a social reserve fund, holding contributions of grain for assistance to members in case of emergency. Over time, as cash replaced kind, the *dhukutis* turned into ROSCAs, intended to generate capital for Thakali businessmen.

During the past fifty years *dhukutis* have spread all over the country. This proliferation is mainly attributable to the increase in business opportunities as the country emerged from 104 years of autocracy and began to open to the world economy. Another factor that encouraged *dhukutis* to multiply was the lack of formal financial institutions. In many rural areas there were no banks or credit unions to offer convenient savings services or broad access to credit.[2]

## From a Culture of Savings to Social Networking

*Dhukutis* thus provided financially excluded people with a means of collecting small savings that could grow with time. As with ROSCAs all over the world, *dhukutis* work on a rotating payout system in which each individual contributes a sum of money at regular intervals and receives a lump sum payout in turn. The organizational structure is highly specific, but also flexible. If a member needs money for her daughter's wedding immediately, she can swap her turn to receive the payout with another. If a member foresees a trip far in the future to attend the birth of a relative, she can negotiate to receive her lump sum at a later turn. And aside from big events, small bits of regular savings add up to purchases of assets such as jewelry, otherwise out of reach.

*Dhukutis* also provide a place for social networking among women. When women meet on a regular basis, they can talk about work and family. Such socialization is not simply for pleasure; it also provides a form of insurance. In the rural and informal economy of Nepal, most people cannot afford medical or asset insurance. The state does not provide unemployment insurance, and there is no comprehensive social security system. In such a scenario people rely on their neighbors, relatives, and friends for help during difficult times. *Dhukutis* thus provide two forms of insurance: a lump sum payout that is available when needed, and a forum for interaction that strengthens the critical social ties among households.

When my mother first heard of *dhukuti*, she was intrigued. Here was something that the subcommittee could pursue with its limited capital, which also included a social aspect. However, when she brought the idea to the subcommittee, members were hesitant. Who would guarantee that people would pay on time? What if someone quit after receiving her payout? This idea seemed to have the potential for more trouble than it was worth.

In order to convince members of the benefits of this new idea, my mother drafted a paper explaining the workings of *dhukuti*. Because the subcommittee was large, she suggested the members form multiple small *dhukutis*, with around fifteen members in each group. The small *dhukutis* would start with each member putting in $25 per month, an amount most women said they would be comfortable to contribute. The subgroups would meet monthly, with different members volunteering to host meetings in their homes and provide lunch to the others.

The subcommittee itself was entered as a member in each of the *dhukutis*; its contribution came from the initial collective investment of $3,500. The first in the sequence to receive a payout was the group itself. For the rest of the members, the sequencing of the payout was determined by a draw, with members free to swap places in the rotation. Such a system required an understanding of other members' needs, a trait that formed the basis of the original women's subcommittee. With the money that the subcommittee was able to generate from its membership in each individual *dhukuti*, it started adult literacy programs and sewing training for women. Women who performed well in sewing traveled to Kathmandu, where they took more training at a public training center; their expenses were paid by the subcommittee.

## From Pocket Savings to Owning a Business

When one of my aunts received her lump sum, she started a small enterprise selling spices. This modest venture was her first attempt at running a business. Spices are generally sold in grocery stores, and she had to network persistently with store owners to make her sales. This process was hard work, but with the encouragement of other group members, she made the business successful, sold it, and started a meat shop. Now she could focus on operating and improving the shop itself, a role that suited her far better. Through this process, my aunt—who had never worked outside her home in her life—gained more than financial independence; she gained self-confidence.

With *dhukuti*, members can learn what other women are doing and what has worked and failed. Women can start their businesses with other members as clients and later expand to the larger market. For women starting their first business, this kind of support system is extremely valuable.

## From *Dhukuti* to a Finance Company with a Social Conscience

Seeing the success of the women's *dhukutis*, the subcommittee leadership suggested turning itself into a cooperative. Thirty-four women contributed a total of $72,000, with a five-year commitment to keep their money in the cooperative. Thus, the Khadgadevi Cooperative was established. Today the cooperative is worth more than half a million dollars.

The Khadgadevi Cooperative now operates like a formal bank, with one main difference: it invests its profits into social development. The cooperative has helped to finance schools and various educational programs and training courses in Bandipur. In December 2008 the cooperative members, who come from various professions, volunteered to conduct a teacher-training program and a dental-health camp. I was there to witness firsthand the solidarity of Bandipur women.

The initial $67 that each member invested in forming the women's development subcommittee was returned to them in five years with interest, as promised. My mother collected the sum, which totaled $480, from her five sisters and created the Chameli Devi Fund in the name of my late grandmother, who had built a secondary school in my hometown, Narayanghat. To this day the school provides free education to approximately two hundred children. The Chameli Devi Fund assists with general maintenance and other expenses.

## The Way Forward

Some ROSCAs in Nepal have failed terribly, leading people to lose faith in this form of informal finance. In spite of risk management precautions such as personal guarantees, members still drop out, causing others to lose money. And as informal institutions, ROSCAs offer no legal protections.

Despite these dangers, my mother took to the idea of *dhukuti*. The associated problems—members dropping out or not paying on time—were social rather than financial. An organization like the women's group, built as it was on strong and lasting social ties, effectively avoided such problems, leading to a suitable environment for a successful *dhukuti*.

When I asked my mother if she would be interested in receiving money from international donors, she proudly replied no. "The women's development subcommittee, Khadgadevi Cooperative, and the Chameli Devi Fund are ours—no one else can claim them," she explained. "This was all achieved through the initiative of local women, and we are very proud of that. It is not that we don't have resources; what we need is to capitalize on them." I asked her what I could do for her organization. "Well," she said, "you can tell other women about us."

## Notes

[1] Hans D. Seibel and Heiko Schrader, "Dhikuti Revisited: From ROSCA to Finance Company," *Savings and Development Quarterly Review* 23, no. 1 (1999): 48–55.
[2] Ibid.

Chapter 3

# From Self-Help Groups to Village Financial Institutions in Bali

*How Culture Determines Finance and Finance Determines Culture*

HANS DIETER SEIBEL

## Cultural and Religious Foundations of Customary Financial Institutions

Preservation of cultural and religious identity is a key concern in Bali. Finance is one of the spheres in which this identity has been challenged. However, this identity will not easily be undermined. Its roots were planted some five hundred years ago by Hindu princes who fled from Java and established a culture of Dharma Hinduism on the island of Bali while incorporating elements of ancient Balinese culture. The result has been an ever-evolving blend of religion and ritual, temple architecture, arts

This article is based on field work conducted in October 2008 as part of a study requested by Promotion of Small Financial Institutions (ProFI), a joint project of Deutsche Gesellschaft für Technische Zusammenarbeit (GTZ) GmbH, Bank Indonesia, and Bank Pembangunan Daerah (BPD) Bali; their support is gratefully acknowledged.

and crafts, music and dance, family life and community associations, irrigated rice cultivation and water-user groups, none
of which fit into a single fixed pattern. A fundamental characteristic of Balinese society is its structural fluidity and diversity.[1]

Bali is composed of two systems. One is secular and part of
the overall Indonesian administrative system. The other is based
on customary law. The highest authority of the customary village and the *banjar* is the assembly of residents, which elects
the respective councils and leaders. Communal activities are arranged around the *banjar*, or customary community, with its
temples and assembly hall, where religious and life-cycle ceremonies take place.[2]

## Financial Institutions at the *Banjar* Level

Every *banjar* has a large variety of groups,[3] and among them
are savings and credit groups.[4] Until the 1970s these groups were
ubiquitous, but quite relaxed about financial discipline. As Holloh
noted in Lodtunduh, Gianyar district: "Borrowers had to pay
monthly interest but were only required to repay the loan principal when the *banjar* had to finance religious rites or public
expenses. Thus, borrowers often did not know when they had
to repay their debts and faced difficulties in repaying the principal in a lump sum when they were asked to do so."[5]

Lodtunduh is an administrative village comprising two customary villages with ten *banjar*. Many of its residents specialize
in wood carving and handicrafts. As their businesses expanded,
so did their demand for credit. Without financial discipline, the
savings and credit groups began facing serious difficulties. Potential solutions came from two quarters. The first was the Credit
Union Coordinating Office in Jakarta, which offered guidance.
Credit unions could have become a model for the moderniza-
tion of informal groups, but they were considered a foreign
element and thus not accepted. An alternative innovation came
from within Bali itself: building financial institutions similar to
the groups but operating at a larger scale—at the level of the
customary village rather than at the smaller *banjar* level.

## Financial Institutions at the Customary Village Level

The initiative to establish Lembaga Perkreditan Desa (LPDs), customary village-level financial institutions, was taken by the governor of Bali in 1984, with the intention of setting up institutions capable of competing with the rapidly expanding banking sector but integrated into Balinese culture. The village appeared more suitable than the *banjar* to guarantee the economies of scale required. In 1984, the Government of Bali passed a decree, and in 1988 a provincial law, defining the customary village as the owner and operational area of this new institution.

In 1988, the central government also enacted a law on rural banks regulated by the central bank. Existing institutions, including LPDs, were to be converted into rural banks. This change would have greatly reduced the number of LPDs, many of which would have been too small to qualify as a bank. The Government of Bali thus objected, and in 1999 the central bank finally exempted the LPDs.[6]

## The Power of *Krama* and *Karma*

The owner of the LPD is the customary village, more specifically, the indigenous residents, *krama ngarep*. Users are *krama ngarep,* other residents, the customary village and *banjar* as corporate bodies, and community associations. Nonresidents are excluded.

Governance is the responsibility of the customary village, which elects a board of supervisors. Ultimate authority lies with the village and constituent *banjar* assemblies as the owner of the LPD. The chairperson regularly reports to the village council; the customary community heads report to their assemblies. Intimate knowledge of all resident families enables the board to arrive at sound credit decisions and to enforce repayment. The strongest threat in case of default is to call out the defaulter's name before the community at the assembly. This would so greatly shame the family of the delinquent that it is virtually never invoked.

There is yet another, even stronger sanctioning power, representing the spiritual dimension of governance: *karma*. Good as well as bad deeds affect a person's *karma*, in this life and, through reincarnation, in the next. Saving, investing savings or loans to the benefit of the family, and repaying loans all positively affect one's *karma*; wasting one's resources and failing to settle debts have a negative impact. It is these two factors—social control by the *krama* and spiritual control by one's *karma*—that explain why the board can be so successful in enforcing repayment, and why physical collateral is rarely seized, if ever.

## If Governance Fails:
## The Role of the Board in the Fall and Rise of an LPD

The nature of good governance is most evident where it has broken down, and the reestablishment of cooperation among board, management and customary village has subsequently turned the LPD around. The following case studies are instructive.

### LPD Kayu Kapas

LPD Kayu Kapas in Bangli district is a tiny institution, established in 2002, which broke down early in its history. The village, located in a remote area, consists of a single customary community with 138 families. The LPD worked reasonably well during the first year. But the board of three farmers was inexperienced and unaware of its responsibilities. Problems started in 2004 when the manager used a substantial amount of the funds for his own purposes. Savers could not withdraw their money, no new loans were issued, and borrowers refused to repay. The district guidance agency, established by the Government of Bali, kept visiting the LPD but failed to revive it.

The turn-around came in May 2007 when the guidance agency invited a well-functioning neighboring LPD to instruct the board about its responsibilities. Without changes in composition, the board convinced the manager and the borrowers to repay their debts. With the help of a six-month loan from another LPD, Kayu Kapas resumed operations. By August 2008 its total assets had increased by 85 percent over the December levels, savings had more than doubled, there were no arrears, and net profit had risen from about $263 to about $505.

The case of LPD Kayu Kapas shows how a young LPD can break down if the board is not aware of its responsibilities. It also shows that, with proper guidance and instruction, a non-functioning board can be turned around, revitalizing a non-performing LPD, restoring confidence, achieving full repayment of arrears despite an extended period during which the LPD was practically closed, and returning to profitability—all this in a very small and remote village normally considered unsuitable for a financial institution of its own. The initiative to revitalize the LPD came from the guidance agency, but only after a delay of three years. The key instrument in bringing about change was the assistance from a well-functioning neighboring LPD.

### LPD Kapal Mengui

LPD Kapal Mengui in Badung district is one of the larger LPDs in Bali, serving a village of eighteen customary communities with 2,275 families. Established in 1990, the LPD functioned well for four years, but then it ran into problems. Manual record-keeping led to errors and eventually to fraud. The board failed to step in, and the village lacked experience running an LPD. The guidance agencies lacked clearly defined tasks and failed to intervene. By 1996 the LPD had accumulated losses of over eight hundred dollars.

In October 1997 a new board was elected, including two board members with financial experience. Immediately the new board acted to revitalize the LPD. It mobilized technical assistance from the guidance agency and the development bank and brought in the customary administration of the village and the customary communities. These local and authoritative bodies defined the responsibilities of the board members and reintroduced adherence to the regulations: "We took a social approach, because the problem was in the community, and we addressed the *krama* at the *banjar* meetings." With full support from the leadership throughout the village, they solved the delinquency problem and recapitalized the LPD with new savings. By the end of 1997, the LPD was again turning a profit; it has remained profitable ever since. In 2002 the LPD modernized its operations through computerization, adopted an operational handbook, and moved to a new building.

The case of LPD Kapal Mengui shows that even in a village with good potential and several years of good performance, an LPD can collapse through fraud and delinquency if the board does not function, the village authorities do not step in, and external supervision is ineffective. The crucial factor in failure was poor governance, just as good governance was decisive in fixing the LPD. Once a new board with a high level of competence and motivation was elected, the LPD was revitalized amazingly fast. The guidance agency and development bank also played a role, but only after the board took strong steps to secure recovery. It so happened that the turn-around took place at the time of the monetary crisis of 1997/98, when the banking sector collapsed. LPD Kapal Mengui, like other LPDs, reported no significant negative effects of the crisis.

### LPD Gelgel

LPD Gelgel in Klungkung serves a village of twenty-eight *banjar* with 2,441 families. Besides agriculture and livestock, there is a multitude of home industries. The LPD was established in 1988 and functioned well for ten years. The situation changed rather abruptly in 1999. Eighty percent of the portfolio fell into arrears. The downfall of the LPD was attributed to a lack of communication and coordination between management and staff, but it is not clear what led to this situation. The management did not insist rigorously on repayment, and there were cases of fraud. The board did not intervene.

The initiative to take action came from two people who had retired from a bank and returned to the village. One became a manager, the other one a board member. The board and management took a "family approach" to solve the problem of non-performing loans, attending *banjar* meetings and convincing defaulters to repay their loans. Everyone repaid, sometimes after rescheduling, and collateral was never confiscated. In revamping the LPD staff, the board and the manager also took a family approach: retaining the staff, insisting on hard work and discipline, introducing good banking practices, and tightening the rules. The board also established a close relationship with two well-performing LPDs, which served as role models and acted as consultants and trainers.

The board of LPD Gelgel succeeded in restoring trust, turning the losses into profits, and the LPD continued to grow every year through 2007. A beautiful new building is currently under construction, fully financed from the group's own resources, right next to the market and the largest temple of Gelgel. The case of LPD Gelgel demonstrates how a committed new governance team can restore trust and achieve full repayment of overdue loans using a soft approach without ever taking recourse to seizing collateral.

Two lessons emerge from these case examples, one pertaining to governance, the other to supervision. While any LPD risks falling into disarray, a motivated and committed board, whether newly elected or reoriented, can revitalize an LPD in an amazingly short period of time. Good governance, with effective control over management, is absolutely crucial.

In none of the case studies has information about poor performance been followed by instantaneous action. While monitoring and reporting are effective, supervision is not. There is no coordination among the various agencies, and there are no instruments of enforcement of regulations. The family approach works well under conditions of good governance. But once governance fails, a similarly soft approach to supervision does not work. Evidently, as in any modern financial system, there are limits to the effectiveness of internal control by *krama* and *karma*. These factors must be supplemented by external supervision and the power of enforcement. Finding a Balinese way of achieving effective external supervision continues to be a challenge to the stakeholders.

## Growth and Outreach of LPDs
## Lead to Economic and Social Impact

By June 2008 LPDs were present in about 95 percent of the customary villages in Bali. Statistically, outreach to the 834,000 families of Bali is virtually universal, though there are regional disparities.

Such massive diffusion has led to changes in Balinese society. There is agreement among the LPD board members and managers that the LPD has a pronounced economic impact. There is now virtually total access to financial services for the whole population of the village—including the poor—at minimal client transaction costs. The LPD serves men and women, without discrimination. The majority of depositors, and many of the borrowers, are women. In many cases men borrow the money and their wives put it to use.

Additionally, the accumulation of savings and access to credit at competitive interest rates has contributed to income smoothing and the purchase of household durables. The LPD has also had a significant impact on local business by increasing the self-financing capacity of small and microenterprises, and increasing access to credit. This access has facilitated self- and debt-financed business start-ups; it has also led to the expansion of existing businesses and to innovation.

Income and employment have increased. Direct employment by the LPDs amounts to seven thousand, or five employees per LPD. There are also indirect income and employment effects through farm and non-farm small enterprises financed through the LPD. The extent of such effects calls for further study.

In addition to direct contributions from profits into a village development fund and a social fund, the LPD has enabled the village and community administrations—which are nonformal entities with little access to formal finance—to accumulate resources, pay their staff and finance public investments. The LPD has also improved the social welfare of the families in various ways: families are able to acquire more livestock; more families are now in a position to pay for higher education of their children; housing has been improved; and access to finance has created new opportunities for the less-fortunate generally. Also, in case of emergencies, families are either able to finance resulting shortfalls and expenses from their savings or to have access to emergency credit.

## Conclusion

The LPD has emerged as a strong and efficient microfinance institution. It has almost fully replaced the former indigenous savings and credit groups that operated at the *banjar* level. Yet, financial institutions at the customary community level have not disappeared. Registered savings and credit cooperatives have been spreading in recent years. In addition, there are many self-help groups established by the Family Planning Board. Large numbers of voluntary associations continue to exist in the customary communities. In all villages visited these associations are reported to save in and to borrow from the LPD. This finding also applies to the cooperatives and many of the self-help groups.

Access to financial services for all has become reality in Bali. The LPD has made a substantial contribution to this achievement, bringing financial services within reach of everyone. At the same time, other, smaller types of financial institutions have come into existence, indicating that there is still a need for self-organized financial services on a very small scale that is not adequately fulfilled by larger institutions, not even those at the village level.

The LPD has given new strength to the customary village. The LPD gives support to the village temples and ceremonies as the center of religious and cultural life in Bali. Large LPDs have directly contributed to village economic development, particularly by supporting infrastructure projects. The LPD enables everyone to make use of the opportunities created by the economic development of Bali. Yet, as village-level institutions, there are limits to the loan demands to which they can respond. Addressing these limitations may require linkages with banks, which may extend larger loans to customers based on their track record at the LPD.

## Notes

[1] Clifford Geertz. "Form and Variation in Balinese Village Structure," *American Anthropologist* 61 (1959): 1010–11.

[2] Clifford Geertz, *Local Knowledge: Further Essays in Interpretive Anthropology* (New York: Basic Books, 1983); Detlev Holloh, *Microfinance in Indonesia: Between State, Market, and Self-Organization* (Hamburg: LIT Verlag, 1998), 177.

[3] Geertz, "Form and Variation in Balinese Village Structure," 1000.

[4] Holloh, *Microfinance in Indonesia*, 177.

[5] Ibid., 214.

[6] Detlev Holloh, *LPD—Lembaga Perkreditan Desa. ProFI Baseline Survey* (Jakarta: GTZ, 2000): 22–24.

Chapter 4

# On an Informal Frontier

*The ASCAs of Lower Assam*

ABHIJIT SHARMA AND BRETT HUDSON MATTHEWS

## Introduction

"*Xonchoi xamitis* [ASCAs] are a way of life for us," says Pronob, a group member from the village of Khakhrisal. *Xonchois* are integral to rural life in many parts of Lower Assam, a region of North East India. Their membership includes villagers young and old, male and female. Today these groups dominate the financial landscape of most parts of rural Assam. In Assamese, they are called *xonchoi xamitis*. *Xonchoi* means "savings," and *xamitis* means "committee" or "society," hence *xonchoi xamitis* means a savings committee or society.

Today, a typical household in Lower and Central Assam may belong to several such institutions, which help meet various savings and credit needs. In the absence of access to formal institutions like banks and post offices, these informal arrangements fill an important gap in financial service provision.

For this study two villages were selected for comparative purposes: Mazarpara (near the city of Guwahati) and Khakhrisal (more remote, on the northern bank of the Brahmaputra River). *Xonchoi* members and leaders were interviewed in both. The *xonchois* in these villages were surveyed to capture a snapshot of the local ASCA system, focusing on individual groups but also on supporting institutions and infrastructure.

*Xonchoi xamitis* in Assam thrive in an area that forms a roughly two hundred kilometer radius around the largest city of the region, Guwahati. Like much of Lower Assam, this poor, densely populated region supplies labor, materials, goods, and services to Guwahati.[1] The density of *xonchois* drops considerably in the remoter hill areas surrounding this region. Besides agriculture, the rural non-farm sector is very vibrant here, with many thriving microenterprises in manufacturing and services. A detailed 1999–2000 survey of the rural non-farm sector in the district of Kamrup found 167,300 microenterprises, employing 418,000 people.[2]

## The *Xonchois* in Lower Assam

The origins of *xonchois* in this area are not well documented. Their members suggest that they may have started around thirty or forty years ago, growing more rapidly over the past two decades. Given the exclusive nature of the formal financial sector, *xonchois* help people accumulate lump sums of money to meet a range of needs.[3]

There appears to be a vibrant movement of informal financial intermediaries, involving people all across the region. Preliminary surveys indicate that the groups are mostly ASCAs, with very few ROSCAs. In some areas sophisticated ASCAs make independent decisions about life-cycles and increase their scope and depth of outreach by providing more products and options to their members. Different parts of the region appear to be at different levels of evolution. Numerous permutations and combinations on the familiar ASCA model have led to a diversity of savings products.

## Introduction to the Surveyed Villages

The two villages selected are from the region of Lower Assam where *xonchois* are predominant. The study covered all of Mazarpara village and a portion of Khakhrisal village. The village of Mazarpara is only fifty kilometers from Guwahati, the largest town of the North East Region of India. Mazarpara is also adjacent to the bustling market town of Chaygaon, which is home to two formal bank branches. Due to its proximity to the region's largest city, Mazarpara is more prosperous than Khakhrisal. Literacy rates are also higher. The area has a vibrant silk-farming industry that plays a key role in female livelihoods.

Khakhrisal is on the northern bank of the Brahmaputra River, deep in the countryside and much further from Guwahati. The area is economically less active and has both lower literacy rates and lower household mobility.

*Xonchois* are ubiquitous in both of these villages. On average, a household belongs to four or more groups. The size of the groups averages twenty in Mazarpara, and twenty-six in Khakhrisal. There are more female groups in Mazarpara. In Khakhrisal, group composition is mixed.

## Operations of the *Xonchoi Xamitis*

### Start-up phase

People use *xonchois* to invest their savings and build a "useably large lump sum"[4] by the end of an agreed period. Most *xonchois* start during the months of agricultural surplus (January through April) or in the intermediate months of September through December. Very few groups start during the lean months of May through August.

One *xonchoi* manager remarked: "Our financial year ends on the first of Magh [a period from mid-January to mid-February]. All of our calculations are done then. The people find it easier to repay because of surpluses available in their houses."

### Contribution amounts

In Mazarpara the average contribution per member per month is 51.6 rupees (about $1), compared with $2.14 in Khakhrisal. The study found that the preferred range is between one and two dollars per month, but the members of one group contribute about ten dollars

Households with higher income streams are allowed to hold more than one savings "share," which can be taken in multiples of the group's base rate. Thus, if a member decides to take three shares in a group that uses $1 per month as their base savings rate, then her contribution will be $3 per month. This type of flexibility makes *xonchois* more inclusive than other financial-service providers in a village and may therefore attract more members.

### Adaptation to seasonality

The cash flows of most households in these villages are highly seasonal. In addition to timing group start-ups during periods of surplus, members manage their contributions in other ways to minimize the impact of seasonality.

Some members want to contribute more than the base rate during the surplus months because they cannot sustain that amount later. Some *xonchois* permit initial "top-ups" over and above the regular savings contribution rate. Later, the members follow the regular savings pattern. Almost half the *xonchois* offer this option, and the average size of the top-up is approximately $2. This ASCA feature allows households to increase their savings during surplus months without the challenge of sustaining it later, when their incomes decline.

In Khakhrisal, *xonchoi* members are allowed to convert missed contributions into loans during the lean months. This scheme is allowed only for two months, after which the member must repay.

### Formal-sector linkages

In Mazarpara, six *xonchois*—a quarter of the *xonchois* in the area—have managed to develop linkages with banks and post offices, but only one has been able to do so in Khakhrisal. These linkages are possible because some *xonchois* in Mazarpara have evolved into semi-permanent institutions capable of managing long-term savings accounts on behalf of their members. These groups are looking for more secure, long-term savings, even though returns are lower than normally received from ASCAs. This situation may be because they have independent auditors, who go through the groups' books annually (more on that below).

## Xonchoi *product types*

ASCAs generally have one savings product: a "recurring deposit" lasting throughout its life span, which in turn finances one loan product. Increasing the operating life span of ASCAs is a key to delivering more useful financial products to members. For example, the village-based "credit unions" in rural Germany in the nineteenth century were financed by farmers' savings. Even though these tiny banks had an average of only ninety-five members each, 21 percent of their loans were for periods exceeding ten years, while only 9 percent were for periods of less than one year.[5] Much of this money financed infrastructure such as wells, irrigation equipment, land, or machinery—assets and endeavors that are impossible to finance with short-term funds.

Similarly, the members in these villages in Assam may have chosen to extend their *xonchoi* life spans because they want to increase the scope of products available. In addition to generating more useful agricultural loans, a longer group life span can also generate more useful savings products that can finance long-term savings goals, such as high school or university education, home renovation, marriage of daughters, or retirement. Longer group life spans also permit longer product life, which makes both savings products and loan products more valuable to members. In these villages there was a significant relationship between the range of products delivered and the life span of the *xonchoi*.

The extension of *xonchois*' lives has led groups to develop new products that build on the basic format. Due to their longer life spans, the *xonchois* of Mazarpara are able to offer longer-term fixed and recurring-term deposits as well as longer-term loans to their members. In Khakhrisal, where group life spans are still relatively short, more than ninety-five of the *xonchois* offer only the classic short-term recurring deposit.

Unlike the standard ASCA, which is based on a regular recurring deposit, four of the twenty-eight *xonchois* of Mazarpara provide a time-deposit service to their members for terms ranging from twelve to twenty-four months. These specialized *xonchois* take a lump sum contribution at their start date, usually in the surplus months of January through March. To avoid complicating their record-keeping and increasing internal control risks, they do not accept subsequent deposits within these specialized ASCAs.

These products are generally offered in different ASCAs. That is, if group members participating in a short-term, recurring deposit scheme want to invest surplus funds in a term deposit, the members create a new *xonchoi* for the purpose. Normally, the short-term *xonchois* break during the surplus months. If there is a surplus after payment of all the dues, this money is rotated as a one-time lump-sum contribution. In Khakhrisal, where ASCA life spans are shorter, the product line remains more traditional.

### Performance in savings accumulation

Product diversity and responsiveness to member needs have led to significant savings accumulation in the *xonchois* of these villages. Total savings of the members in *xonchois* in Mazarpara and Khakhrisal are estimated at $10,609 and $9,652, respectively. Average savings per member are $19.65 for Mazarpara and $19.16 for Khakhrisal. Per member savings in the long-term *xonchois* are much higher, up to $164.71 in one case.

Since each household belongs to an average of seven *xonchois* in Mazarpara and four in Khakhrisal, at any point in time an average household has around $137 (Mazarpara) or $77 (Khakhrisal) invested in them. This is a considerable sum compared to the amount saved in the self-help groups (SHGs) of the region. SHGs are typically promoted by various agents of the Government of India, as well as by state banks and NGOs. The average savings per SHG in Assam are estimated to be about $110, though data on savings per member household are unavailable.[6] Local households are saving, it would seem, a great deal less in SHGs than in *xonchois*.

## Xonchoi Financial Systems

### Life span of the xonchois

The average life of the *xonchois* in Mazarpara is twenty-nine months, while in Khakhrisal it is slightly less (twenty-four months).

However, the difference in relative life spans widens considerably when the eight ASCAs with indefinite life spans in Mazarpara are included.

Even the short-term *xonchois* of Assam have fairly long life spans by worldwide ASCA standards. There are none with life spans of less than twelve months. It is possible that the high levels of social capital in North East India have facilitated the extension of term periods. Other factors, including their independent auditors and managers, may have also helped to extend the ASCA life-cycle.

Across the two villages, six *xonchois* had agreed to a life span of twelve months, twenty-four more were operating for up to two years, and another seven for up to three years. Two more had agreed to life spans of between three to five years, while eight had established no fixed date for breaking.

Mazarpara's "open-ended" *xonchois* have no fixed terminal date. All of these groups had already been in existence for between three and ten years when the team visited. These groups periodically divert some of their accumulated capital to a bank or postal savings account. Providing one of the most valuable services in informal finance, these groups are building up long-term capital to help members meet their long-term financial needs.

### Informal auditors

Auditors help ensure transparency in the accounts even after amounts begin to grow, decreasing the need for frequent distribution of assets. A corps of independent auditors has emerged in Mazarpara. Usually schoolteachers and educated young people, they help groups lengthen their life spans, even helping some evolve into open-ended *xonchois*. In Mazarpara there are six regular auditors and at least four others available when needed. The auditors have a vested interest in the quality of their work, since most of them are also members of the groups and own multiple shares in them.

Auditors do their work annually, and the results are orally disseminated to group members. Some groups also assign different members to maintain asset and liability records, which are reconciled quarterly.

**Xonchoi** *managers*

Managers help in maximizing returns over longer periods of time and play a major role in maintaining group quality. They must attract "star borrowers" to the group: members able to take out and repay the loans reliably and punctually. Over time, these managers gain experience and sharpen their skills. Given their importance, the village of Khakhrisal has developed professional managers, who are paid for their services.

One example is Krishna Talukdar from the Lower Assam region, the heartland of the indigenous Assamese. Krishna began as his group's secretary when it had only a handful of members and the monthly contribution was $0.96 per member. Recognizing his value, the group offered him starting pay of forty cents per month for his services.

Twenty years of savings later, the group has thirty-four members, with a monthly contribution of just under two dollars. Success is owed to Krishna, who earns a small but important profit for his services. The success and popularity of his ASCA results from his arrangement with the group to ensure that all the funds are actively working during the year. When there are cash shortages in the village, almost all the funds are used by members, who borrow from the ASCA at 5 percent a month. After the harvest, however, the village is flush with cash, and, with few demands from members for loans, there is a risk of new contributions sitting idle. By agreement with the members, Krishna borrows these funds at the same rate and lends them at his own risk to non-members. He usually charges about 10 percent a month and can keep these loans active until the ASCA dissolves. This generates significant extra income for him. Talukdar is also an energetic saver who contributes a substantial portion of the revenue from his small tea-and-snack stall to the five ASCAs in which he is a member. He has been able, over the years, to build a house with the proceeds.

### System assets and liabilities

Given the complexity of their product offerings and the development of "meso" level informal institutions like *xonchoi* auditors and skilled managers, these villages have developed informal financial "systems." A snapshot of the aggregated assets and liabilities for these systems, segmented by village, is provided in Table 4–1.

### Table 4–1. Xonchoi Financial Systems Compared

| | Mazarpara Nov. 18–20, 2008 | | Khakhrisal Feb. 14–15, 2009 | |
| --- | --- | --- | --- | --- |
| | US$ | % | US$ | % |
| Assets | | | | |
| Cash in hand | 3,747 | 24% | 44 | 0.4% |
| Cash in bank | 1,873 | 12% | | 0.0% |
| Term deposit in bank | 1,608 | 10% | 41 | 0.3% |
| Term deposit in post office | 196 | 1% | | 0.0% |
| Loans outstanding | 8,221 | 53% | 12,583 | 99.3% |
| Total | 15,644 | 100% | 12,668 | 100.0% |
| | | | | |
| Liabilities and Equity | | | | |
| Savings/equity contributions | 10,297 | 66% | 9,368 | 74% |
| Retained earnings | 5,347 | 34% | 3,298 | 26% |
| Total | 15,644 | 100% | 12,666 | 100% |

It is clear from Table 4–1 that *xonchois* have evolved in different directions in the two villages. In Khakhrisal the classic "recurring deposit plus short-term credit" formula remains reasonably intact. In Mazarpara, *xonchoi* life spans are extending and new savings products are emerging. Mazarpara (which is closer to Guwahati) is more exposed to government subsidy schemes. Government subsidies to SHGs are distorting credit markets in the area and leading people to form groups to secure easy credit. As a result, *xonchois*, which are formed more to provide secure investments than easy credit, are shying away from lending in the local market and moving much of their capital to the safety of more formal institutions like banks and post offices.

In Khakhrisal lower default risk (only three cases of default were reported during the survey) has encouraged *xonchois* to focus on higher returns. There are, however, some signs of *xonchois* pursuing longer-term deposits here, too.

## Conclusion

*Xonchois* are vital institutions for rural people in the plains of Assam, providing both savings and credit. These groups are appealing because they are based on savings and driven by members' needs. The increasing size of the investments flowing through them and their expanding membership suggest they have earned public confidence. They are simple, flexible, and adaptable, yet robust and sustainable.

A recent study on savings in the North East by *MicroSave*[7] shows the high premium placed by rural households on savings attributes like security and return. These *xonchois* are providing members with safer savings, replacing the higher but riskier returns of informal investments like livestock and jewelry with a range of more predictable, lower-risk financial products.

In Mazarpara the ASCAs have extended their life spans and have in some cases achieved functional permanence. They credit their success to the introduction of a new meso-level institution— the informal external auditor who helps ensure transparency and reduces shareholder risk. Auditors have also helped these groups initiate savings linkages with banks and post offices.

The relationship between ASCA health and the presence of formal-sector financial institutions is an interesting and complex one. While it might be assumed that ASCAs will emerge largely where formal financial systems are absent, the *xonchoi* system in Mazarpara may be stronger precisely because of its proximity to formal finance. The local financial system has received large injections of government subsidies in recent years. Poor repayments in some SHGs have made ASCAs cautious about lending—a factor that may have influenced the emergence of many savings links with the formal sector and the observed extension of local *xonchoi* life spans.

Nevertheless, in these villages everybody knows who the good *xonchoi* managers are, who the good members are, and who the good record-keepers are. In Mazarpara they also know which auditors to trust. Setting up a new ASCA involves little more than identifying reliable members with a shared financial services need. The line separating this complex mix of informal shared understandings and practices from a permanent institution is thin and thinning.

This study was quick and preliminary, and it has raised more questions than answers:

- What are the main factors affecting the current distribution and speed/patterns of diffusion of ASCAs in different subregions and villages of the North East? What are the relative levels of social capital or economic vibrancy, literacy rates, displacement/links to informal sources of funds, proximity to formal financial institutions, length of time since ASCA technology was first introduced, and so on?

- What meso-level institutions are most important to *xonchoi* financial systems, and how do they emerge?
- Are there recurring characteristic patterns of development in *xonchoi* financial systems and the *xonchois* that compose them?
- Globally, the risk of fraud and "elite capture"—more powerful members of a community taking over the operations and benefits of a group—grows as the life span of an ASCA increases and its common fund increases in size. How are transparency and accountability maintained in *xonchois,* given low literacy rates among members? What factors have allowed the *xonchois* of Mazarpara effectively to mitigate the threats to their common funds?
- While governments and development experts debate how to link banks to villagers for delivery of credit, the *xonchois*, their managers, and their auditors are earning public trust. They are also helping members plan for the future by initiating linkages with banks for savings. *Xonchois* are sustainably delivering credit products with greater seasonal flexibility than many offered by mainstream microfinance institutions. And they are sustainably delivering savings products, which microfinance institutions are not typically doing at all. So one final question might be this: Is there anything the wider field of microfinance can learn from these pioneers?

## Notes

[1] Sa-Dhan, *Microfinance in the North East Region: Expanding Outreach to the Underserved Region* (New Delhi, India: Sa-Dhan, 2007).

[2] Indian Institute of Bank Management, "District Potential Survey of Rural Non Farm Sector—Kamrup District" (Guwahati: IIBM, 2000).

[3] Abhijit Sharma, *Banking Industry in the North East Region of India: Making It Financially More Inclusive* (Shillong: North East Council, Government of India, 2009).

[4] This term is from Stuart Rutherford, *The Poor and Their Money: An Essay about Financial Services for Poor People* (New Delhi, India: Oxford University Press, 2000); Rutherford's concepts help shape the foundation of this chapter.

[5] Timothy Guinnane, "Cooperatives as Information Machines: German Rural Credit Cooperatives, 1883–1914," *Journal of Economic History* 61, no. 2 (2001): 366–89.

[6] Data for Assam from the "State-Level Bankers' Committee Report, 2005–6," State Bank of India, Guwahati, Assam (2006). Data for other states compiled from the corresponding State-Level Bankers' Committee reports for the other North Eastern states.

[7] Madhurantika Moulick, "Understanding and Responding to the Savings Behavior of Poor People in the North East of India," AMAP microREPORT 103 (2008).

Despite the Haitian earthquake of 2010, which devastated the financial activities of much of Port-Au-Prince, Brave Warriors, a savings group of twenty members, continues to meet every Thursday evening.

# PART 2

---

# NOW THEY NEED US
# (OR DO THEY?)

This part moves on from customary groups to promoted ones. In contrast to customary groups, which form on their own, promoted groups form with the help of trained experts from the outside. Customary groups do not need us; they just do it. Promoted groups do need us; they do not just do it.

However, we do run into some persistent questions: If so many millions of people, particularly poor women, have for so many hundreds of years formed themselves into savings groups, why is there any need for promotion at all? Should we not get out of the way and let them get on with it? Is savings-group promotion anything more than another way in which donors and their agents justify their jobs? Are promoted groups any better than customary ones? Before we examine the ways in which groups are promoted, and by whom, we must briefly address these questions.

First, and most obvious, not every poor person who might benefit from membership in a savings group is a member. In some places, for a variety of reasons, there are very few groups. Even in places where groups proliferate, many people—particularly the poorest—are not members.

Second, the methods and systems of group and money management that are promoted have been carefully designed, and are still being improved, on the basis of worldwide experience.

Simply put, these methods are usually better than those of customary systems. Steel boxes with triple locks, formal procedures, simple recording systems that illiterate people can use, total transparency—all these features save time and help to reduce loss and theft.

Perhaps even more important, rigid procedures that everyone understands reduce the space for disagreement. Like marriage contracts that lay down who gets what in the event of divorce, these procedures not only guide the members on how to deal with disagreements, they also reduce the number of issues about which people can disagree.

Finally, although one of the strengths of these savings groups is their independence from outsiders of any kind, the members may decide that they should open a bank account or collaborate in some other way with other groups or institutions. Better, more formal records can help groups to establish their credentials and can improve their chances of getting bank loans, if the members want them.

We can probably accept, therefore, that there is a good case for promoting these groups. What do the papers in this section tell us about the promotion process?

Chapter 5 is unusual; it is an interview with Moira Eknes, the modest Norwegian woman who can in some sense be considered the pioneer of modern savings-group promotion. One of the editors of this book was a microfinance "expert" who was working in Maradi in Niger when Moira Eknes was quietly engaged in this remarkable work. Only much later has he come to appreciate fully the significance of what she was doing.

Mabel Guevara and Bridget Bucardo Rivera describe in Chapter 6 their experience of a joint project undertaken in El Salvador by three big international NGOs to learn about the group formation and management process. This article charts their early discoveries as they learn about savings groups.

Organizations that promote groups ordinarily do so in settled communities, where the members can meet regularly and conveniently. In Chapter 7 Matthew Griffith shows how savings groups can also prosper in far harsher circumstances, among mobile pastoralists in the northern deserts of East Africa.

Most agencies that promote groups have focused on developing autonomous groups, which can survive and prosper without being linked to any institution, least of all a bank. In Chapter 8 Girija and N. Srinivasan describe the Indian self-help-group program, which takes a very different approach. It deliberately seeks to do the opposite—to link groups to banks. The members are mainly motivated not by their desire to save and borrow from the group's accumulated savings, but by the promise of a loan from a bank, which may also be "sweetened" by a government subsidy. Over five million of these self-help groups—with perhaps seventy five million mostly female members—have taken out bank loans after an initial qualifying period of member saving. The Indian program is the world's largest microfinance activity and clearly merits recognition.

Chapter 5

# Revisiting the Early Days of CARE's Savings Groups

## Interview with Moira Kristin Eknes, Village Savings and Loan Associations (VSLA) Program Originator

INTERVIEW CONDUCTED BY KRISTIN HELMORE

Moira Kristin Eknes has worked with CARE in various posts since 1990, first as a project manager in Niger and currently as African regional program senior advisor at CARE Norway head-quarters. In July 2008, Niger's Ministry of Territorial and Community Development honored Eknes's work on savings groups with an Official Certificate of Accomplishment. Kristin Helmore conducted this interview by email and phone with Moira Eknes to learn about the origins of CARE's VSLA methodology.

**Kristin Helmore (KH):** Where did you first launch savings groups MMD [Mata Masu Dubara, or Women on the Move] in Niger?

**Moira Eknes (ME):** The first six villages were in the Guidan Roumji district in Maradi department. Maradi town is the second largest city in Niger, about 670 kilometers east of Niamey, the capital city.

The project was initially meant to last only for two or three years. The funding came from the Norwegian Centre Party's Women Association's participation in the telethon in 1989 for

Women in the Third World. But in 1992 the project was integrated into CARE Norway's frame agreement with NORAD, and thus secured long-term funding, and we expanded into more villages in the same district.

**KH:** What was the main source of livelihood in the area where you worked?

**ME:** Subsistence agriculture: millet, sorghum, some maize, dry-season gardening, all combined with some animal husbandry. Married women tried to supplement these with some kind of income-generating activity, but they often found it difficult since they had problems keeping the activities going due to lack of working capital.

**KH:** What were the results of poverty?

**ME:** High illiteracy rates, bad nutrition levels, lack of information, high infant and maternal mortality, coupled with the lack of access to safe drinking water. This is a polygamous society, and women had to work most days of the week on the family field but had no control over the harvest. All the same, women were responsible for feeding themselves and their own children from whatever they could produce on the small plots given to them at marriage. From our first survey we found that, on average, women spent up to six hours a day fetching water and firewood.

**KH:** Where did the savings-group approach come from at the time you started the work? Was it experimental? What was the reaction of the first group of women when you suggested they start a savings group?

**ME:** The approach was very experimental. The concept paper I was handed as an intern during the first year of project management in Niger did focus on economic security through resource mobilization, but there was little in it in terms of methodology and proposed activities.

The women were already familiar with tontines (ROSCAs), so the idea was not completely strange to them. Mind you, we did not have a methodology when we started; we sort of developed it along with the women of the first groups.

**KH:** How many women were in these groups, and were they doing any kind of economic activities?

**ME:** The first groups were quite large, as we started with one group per village—forty to sixty members sometimes—too large to handle. After a while we decided to split them, and the average number was around thirty per group. About 98 percent of members were illiterate. Most groups did not have even one literate member.

Most of the participants were engaged in some kind of irregular income generating activity: petty trade, peanut-oil making, sale of cakes or food dishes. Most members were older women, either widows or grandmothers. The younger women came on board later, as men realized that membership in the groups was advantageous to the whole family.

**KH:** Was it difficult to convince the women that they could actually start a savings group with their own money?

**ME:** No, but CARE was running a big microcredit program in Maradi at the time, the Rural Development Bank (BRK). Some of the women expected that they would get access to credit from the BRK—and some of them did—as groups. The BRK previously had only given credit to individuals, and they found it interesting to work with the savings groups, as it saved them time and energy and the individual amounts became more adapted to the individual needs for small amounts. However, the BRK failed in the end and was closed, but savings groups continued and spread.

In fact, it was not difficult to convince the women that they should contribute their own savings; it was with other CARE staff and our government counterparts that we found skepticism and resistance. They really thought that the project was demanding too much of poor women. Even some of the visiting microfinance experts were doubtful when we tried to explain what we did. And, mind you, I did not feel completely convinced in the beginning, but since I did not have a credit line and working capital, which was what they needed and wanted, the savings-group idea was the best solution possible. I feared sometimes that the whole thing was pointless, but the women themselves convinced me otherwise.

**KH:** I was fascinated to see that you "sort of developed the methodology with the women in the first groups." Can you elaborate on how that happened? What were some of the things the women suggested or said they wanted?

**ME:** I cannot recall exactly who suggested what when—the point was that the box, social fund, action audit, delayed reimbursement (only paying interest due), one woman having two "hands" or shares, and so on—all this was developed through discussions in the groups and in our weekly staff meetings, where field agents would exchange what had happened in their groups, any problems, and possible solutions.

The first three field agents I recruited were instrumental in the process. They were from Maradi town, all young women in their late teens or early twenties, with a high school or college education. They were based in the villages, almost like Peace Corps volunteers. They organized the savings and loans groups, and also other activities, such as village sanitation, vegetable gardening, or handicrafts. The savings groups were only one of several activities in the beginning, but after the first evaluation we decided to focus more on the savings and loan group aspect of the project, which had been the most successful.

**KH:** It is fascinating to read about the young field agents you recruited. Did these young women have a problem gaining the respect and trust of older women who were members of the groups?

**ME:** No. Amazingly, they were well respected by the older women, and also by the men in the village. We introduced them to the village authorities first, explaining the ideas of the project, and they were welcomed. They had, of course, been carefully hand picked, so that we were sure that they knew how to behave respectfully in a village context. All in all, they had very good rapport with the people in their villages.

**KH:** Could you describe how the training was carried out, what it consisted of, and how long it lasted?

**ME:** In the beginning the training was not as streamlined as it is now, so we were working with the same groups for several years, but we developed the methodology together with the early groups. After some time we elaborated a more formal training. The first training manual consisted of elements of organizational development, the role and responsibilities of the board and its members, purpose of savings, forms of savings, pros and cons of taking a loan, interest rates and fees, income-generation activities, and the basis for the rules and regulations to guide individual groups to decide on their own rules. An introduction to the local public services, like agriculture and health, was also part of the training.

By the time I left, the training cycle for new groups was fifteen months. Later the program was made more efficient and the cycle was reduced to ten months. Now, in most places it takes between ten to twelve months for group formation and skill adoption.

**KH:** How much did the women save, and how often? Who decided these things?

**ME:** The members in the group agreed on what the weekly amount of savings contribution should be. The individual amounts ranged from the equivalent of two cents to sixty cents, depending on the group. All the members initially contributed the same amount, but some time later we discovered that some women had more "hands"—that is, they saved twice or three times the agreed amount; this is now known as the share system. They got two or three times the amount of interest at the time of sharing the fund. The size of loans they could access did not, at least at the time, depend on their number of hands or shares. Decisions were made in the group meetings with everyone present. The rules were decided by the group and could be changed if the majority of the group agreed.

**KH:** Did the savings earn interest? And if so, that interest money they received must have been generated by the interest paid on loans, right?

**ME:** Yes, and by payment of fines, and other income, like profit from grain speculation that some groups soon began.

**KH:** How did they keep track of the amounts they saved and all the other record-keeping?

**ME:** By memorizing. Since, in principle, everybody should have saved the same at any time (or twice or thrice depending on their number of shares or hands), it was easy. Also, the "bank statement" of the fund was declared at the end of each meeting and checked at the following meeting. Particular members were given the responsibility to remember the various amounts; the amount of savings, amount of interest, loans outstanding, cash in box, solidarity-fund situation, and so on. Some groups used pebbles to remember how many meetings they had already had. This system enabled them to determine total savings and interest by counting the number of pebbles, multiplying that by the number of members or shares, and multiplying that by the amount of one share.

**KH:** Did the women elect a treasurer to keep the money in the box that CARE provided?

**ME:** Yes, typically the board consisted of a treasurer, president, secretary, and two controllers. But the first batch of groups simply had a president. Board functions were developed only in the second year. To start, they kept the money in whatever they found to be a good place—hollowed gourds, bags, enamel pots—and this was kept by the president, or even sometimes the field agent!

However, the box idea came when I was in Rafin Wada discussing group matters with the president. She was telling me that it was difficult for her to turn down requests from her husband or the village chief for loans or gifts, since they knew she had access to cash. She even said that she herself had had to contribute money to the group fund before the next meeting, to make sure the amount was the same as at the previous meeting's closure. So I asked whether a box with three padlocks would ease the burden of the cash holder, and she said yes, that would be a good idea. Ever since then, the groups have had a physical box in which to store the cash. . . . In the beginning CARE paid for it, but as the numbers of groups grew, the groups started to pay for the boxes themselves.

**KH:** How often could the women withdraw their savings?

**ME:** Only in what some call action audits—no individual withdrawals. The groups decided when this action audit should take place, usually before the agricultural season, or the start of the school year.[1]

**KH:** What kinds of things did they use their savings for?

**ME:** Among other uses, paying for agricultural inputs like seeds and fertilizer, school tuition, the purchase of goats, or transporting their goods to market. They also funded baptismal ceremonies and marriages of their daughters.

**KH:** What was the repayment rate? Did they repay on time with interest? I assume these loans were used for their income-generating activities. Can you give a few examples of these activities?

**ME:** They usually paid back on time. If not, they paid the interest and extended the loan for another term, usually a month. The social pressure to pay back was, and is, very strong in these groups. Borrowers usually paid 10 percent interest per month for a loan.

**KH:** How did the insurance element work?

**ME:** Most groups had what we called a social fund; this is a separate fund, made up of one-time contributions and managed separately from the savings and loans fund but kept in the box as well. Most often the social fund provided cash assistance in case of emergencies and was paid back on different terms from normal loans. Usually you could claim it outside the meeting, but you had to have the three key holders' and the president's approval.

**KH:** I saw a document about BRK that said that Niger is a particularly difficult environment to do microfinance. So it is ironic that you started the project in Niger. Can you comment on why this happened?

**ME:** Well, the funding was there for women in Niger before there was a detailed and elaborate project document. But, yes, many microfinance experiences had failed and people were very skeptical, not only of microfinance institutions but of the formal banking system as well, which of course had limited outreach anyway. Actually, regarding the action audit or annual distribution of the group fund—this practice came about because some of the groups had mobilized quite substantial amounts that surpassed their need for credit. Three groups of one of the field agents decided they would put their surplus funds into a postal savings account—and our field agent helped them do so. Unfortunately, the Postal Bank froze the funds that year and the groups could never recover their savings. Experiences like this have over time led to strong skepticism about formal financial-services institutions in Niger, so a system in which they feel in control is more acceptable to people, I suppose.

**KH:** You said, "I did fear sometimes that the whole thing was pointless—but the women themselves convinced me otherwise."

**ME:** It was maybe a bad way of putting it, but the human conditions in the area and the burdens on women seemed too great. The fact that we did not provide credit, or anything else tangible other than training, made me feel that I and the project had little to offer. But the women were very eager—and convinced me by their patience, availability, and ability to mobilize meager resources that it all did have a positive effect on them. Again, what they said was most important—their being able to save, to open their minds, and to feel solidarity among themselves as women.

I remember when we had a "surprise" visit from the country director in CARE-Togo at a time when there was a political crisis in Togo and staff was evacuated. The director came to the office one day and said he wanted to visit my project that very same day. He went out with a driver to one of the villages where one of the field agents—according to schedule—would be having a group meeting. He came back completely excited and said that he had found the meeting and "all the members of the group were present . . . and they didn't even know that I was coming!" He said he had rarely experienced such enthusiasm and commitment with participants in other projects.

**KH:** How did the idea of savings groups spread to other villages?

**ME:** People visiting from other villages saw women in the groups, were inspired by them, and then approached the field agents to ask them to help form their own groups. There were also groups that copied what they had seen in "our villages" without the help of an agent.

**KH:** Please describe an example of "spontaneous replication."

**ME:** Well, I recently learned how savings groups formed in the peri-urban areas of Niamey. In 1999 a teacher from Niamey, Sibitou Boubacar, was visiting the village of Torodi, where her sister was living. She came when her sister was in the savings-group meeting, and observed. Sibitou was impressed by the discipline and the level of resource mobilization in the group, as she herself had tried many times to organize the women in her neighborhood, with no success. Thinking that forming savings groups would be worth an attempt, she contacted CARE in Niamey but was told that the urban area was not part of the target zone. So she got hold of one of the agents and asked every question she could think of and started a group. After a year she had five groups—and CARE at the same time started to realize working in urban areas could be very worthwhile.

In general as soon as a group gets going in a village, it does not take long before another group forms. This phenomenon is why CARE later changed the strategy from using CARE-employed field agents to village-appointed village agents to do the training of groups, in order to ensure sustainability and local competence.

**KH:** Do you have one or two examples of groups creatively adapting the training to meet their own circumstances and needs?

**ME:** Yes. For example, one group offers multiple shares in which one member saves twice or more the weekly minimum amount. If they agree that all members must save 100 francs (about twenty cents) per week, one woman might have two "hands," as they would say, and put in forty cents each week. She would then receive twice the amount at the action audit.

But some groups also share a share, splitting the share 50/50. In the example above, two would each put in fifty francs per week to make a 100 francs. The two women would only occupy one membership, though, and only one of them could take a loan, which they would then split between them. This was not very widespread, but it was a phenomenon discovered to accommodate women who were more vulnerable.

Some groups also invested their collective funds in grain speculation; groups would decide to put some of the savings into buying sorghum or millet, the local staple, and buy it at harvest time when the market was glutted and prices were low. For example, they would buy grain at five dollars a bag and sell it during the lean season when prices were high and make a profit of seven to ten dollars or more per bag.

**KH:** What effect did group membership have on the women psychologically and in terms of their standing in their families and communities?

**ME:** An enormous effect. In the first evaluation we did in 1992, the clear response was that the greatest advantage from group participation was the "broadening of the mind" and the possibility to save—and not to be forced to humiliate yourself by asking for money from your husband, a moneylender, or others. Men reported being impressed with their wives and sisters, and the women told us they had more clout in household decision making as a result of being part of a group.

**KH:** What was the greatest moment of this whole experience for you?

**ME:** I have many good memories, but one day I was in my office in Maradi and in came a village woman whom I had never seen before. She greeted me and told me that she was from a village twenty-five kilometers east of Maradi. She had visited a neighboring village where the village agent was working with one of the savings groups there—and she asked that I allow the village agent to come and help them set up a group in her village as well. Can you imagine? She had walked the twenty-five kilometers just to get us to come to work with her and the women in her village. Also, at some of the first action audits—when the members receive their savings with interest—women who had never seen $15 in their lives, holding it in their hands, knowing that this was their own money—the joy and awe!

The program has continued to develop since its beginning. I have visited Niger many times and spoken with savings-group women who have told me how they have solved various problems in their village. These women describe fixing or installing water pumps and ensuring emergency stocks of grain; some have even been elected to the communal council to defend the interests of women. They also have told me how they have realized the value of education and are thus sending their girls to school.

## Note

[1] Action audits happen once a year, or however often groups decide. Groups return all the cash in the box to members so that each member can physically touch, hold, feel, and see the savings and interest. Some call these group disbursals, distributions, or share-outs.

# Chapter 6

# The Savings Experience

*Catholic Relief Services El Salvador*

MABEL GUEVARA AND BRIDGET BUCARDO RIVERA

## The Project

In October 2008, Catholic Relief Services El Salvador partnered with Caritas (Santiago de María diocese) and CARE El Salvador to start a savings-led microfinance pilot project in the two poorest municipalities of the country—Torola in the region of Morazán, and San Antonio del Mosco in the region of San Miguel. This six-month pilot was intended to explore the possibility of including a savings group component within a three-year, multi-country project to improve rural livelihoods.

## Preparation

Our first step was learning about savings groups ourselves. None of us had had any experience with them. After simple training through which we learned the basics of member-owned-and-operated savings groups, several of us decided to try them out ourselves. Why put rural communities at risk of a bad idea? If savings groups helped us, then we would feel more confident about sharing any "secrets of success" with those who were likely to be far poorer than we were. So we started in our own backyard. We formed our own savings groups with co-workers in the office and with family members at home. In a short time we realized that no matter how small our savings contributions seemed, the funds grew quickly, as did the social bonds within our groups.

We were eager to see how rural community members would respond, and we developed a plan of action for two municipalities that the government had identified as "extremely poor."

## Group Formation and Training

To get communities interested, or even to become aware of the idea of savings groups, we held information meetings. Participants were skeptical. They claimed they had no money to save. We noticed, though, that people did have at least some disposable income, however little it might be.

During one of the first community meetings, Mabel Guevara, one of the authors, asked participants, "How many of you save a portion of your earnings?" No one raised a hand. Participants began to speak out: "How can we save if we can barely survive on the income we have?" Even the local priest argued that the idea of saving was not realistic for the rural poor of El Salvador, who barely scratch a living from subsistence farming, often without enough to pay for family education and health care. But then Mabel asked, "How many of you use a cell phone?" The majority of the participants raised their hands and, looking around, began to laugh. They realized that, although they were poor, they could still make decisions about how to use what money they did have. They could choose, for example, to purchase time on a pre-paid cell phone card or instead to invest it in a savings group.

We conducted ten similar community meetings, speaking with more than 230 rural Salvadorans. We found the men in the communities to be far more resistant than the women to the idea of savings. In one meeting, in which only six of the twenty attendees were women, all of the men rejected the savings-group concept, while all of the women were willing to try it.

Once communities had expressed interest in participating in savings groups, each community elected candidates for promoters who would be responsible for organizing the groups and accompanying the members as they learned to save and administer funds. Eventually, a group of eight promoter candidates participated in a week-long workshop in Chalatenango. The training was led by promoters from savings groups already formed by Oxfam America. From this group of eight female candidates, we chose six to become promoters. We offered a small monthly stipend to each promoter for her efforts to organize and support savings groups.

Once trained, promoters began forming savings groups within their own communities. Groups started to meet, to elect their management committees (president, secretary, and treasurer), and to create their constitutions. The constitutions would allow members to establish how much they would save and the length of time they would operate before disbursing their accumulated cash. They decided when, where, and how often they would meet, and they specified the fines they might charge if members were late to a meeting or missed a savings deposit or loan payment.

After the groups had developed their constitutions, we provided materials to help them manage their funds: a lockable cash box for their savings, several keys to the box, a record-keeping journal, an eraser, a calculator, and two pens. Between meetings one group member would carry the cash box while another carried the cash box keys, thereby ensuring that group funds would be accessed only during meetings.

## Early Progress

After just a few months, 219 people (192 women and 27 men) now participate in savings groups. Savings rates are modest but steady. For example, in Torola, the poorest municipality in El Salvador, bi-weekly savings deposits range from twenty-five cents to one dollar, depending on the financial capacity of group members. Altogether, the groups in San Antonio del Mosco and in Torola have saved over $150.

## Challenges in Implementation

During the preparation phase we realized that family obligations made it difficult for promoters to leave their homes for a full week of training. So we shortened the length of training workshops, and we now try to hold them closer to where promoters live. We also learned that where trainings are held can be just as important as when they are held. For instance, when promoters attended a training at a local hotel, unhappy neighbors sparked rumors that trainees were involved in suspicious activities.

Different kinds of challenges emerged when groups began to form. While visiting group meetings, we observed that some groups had difficulty counting their funds and maintaining clear records. We developed a simple registry book to keep track of member attendance, group and individual savings amounts, cashbox balances, and loan information. We offered a day-long course for promoters, during which we reviewed new tools with them and received their suggestions for improvement.

We also observed that many group members were illiterate, and some were unable to sign their names. If they could not read or write, they could not keep or understand the records; rank and file members would never be able to fill leadership roles in the group. We have since developed, at least in part, memory-based systems to allow records to be kept easily by illiterate members.

## Lessons Learned and Looking Ahead

From the pilot we learned three critical lessons. First, we now know promoter training should take place within the communities. This practice eliminates the need for promoters to leave their home obligations for training and should mute community rumors. Second, we learned that people who cannot read and write need far simpler systems to keep records than our current bookkeeping procedures. Memory-based systems developed in other parts of the world seem like good resources for us. Third, giving group members a chance to practice the collection, disbursal, and counting of money is critical. So is record keeping. Oral repetition and practice with false cash both can help.

In looking forward, one particular area of promise is youth. During the pilot we noticed that the children of the members, some as young as seven, ten, and even four years old, wanted to join savings groups. We decided to experiment with special groups for children and youth; these would meet every two weeks without adults. Children proved to be excited about saving. Some did more chores around the house to make money for their savings groups. Some saved by not purchasing snacks at school. The older teenagers started small trading businesses; they bought something in the town where their secondary school was located and resold it at a profit in their villages.

Uses of savings varied. The teenagers wanted to boost their trading businesses and used savings to purchase more inventory. Some saved for their *quinceañero* (fifteenth birthday), a much celebrated life-cycle event in El Salvador. The younger children saved for birthday presents, to buy shoes, or, in some cases, to buy food.

The youth savings groups had many of the same features as their adult counterparts—regular savings requirements, regular meetings, youth members taking leadership roles, and group-based record keeping (a skill at which the young people proved surprisingly adept). However, we soon learned that we had to make meetings more exciting for young people. Games, stories, and physical movement are critical to spurring and maintaining the interest of young people. With the help of a graphic artist we designed a coloring book. Each book has twenty-four pages, one page per meeting. The drawings are simple, and each illustrates a life lesson. For example, one page shows a son helping his mother with cleaning. Another shows children brushing their teeth. And another shows them washing their hands before a meal. Immediate gratification is also important. Youth want their savings boxes opened and the money disbursed at least every couple of months.

This pilot demonstrated that savings groups hold promise as a way both to instill good financial practices early and to provide children and adolescents with the chance to be members of a group and leaders of a group, good practice for their forthcoming adult roles as participants in civil society.

## Conclusion

Learning, promoting, and implementing savings-led microfinance in rural El Salvador has been a journey both for us and for the rural communities with which we work. The change from skepticism about rural Salvadorans' potential to save to a strong and enthusiastic embrace of the savings methodology has been remarkable. Many rural Salvadorans now believe in their own ability to save, and they are increasing their assets and strengthening bonds and trust within their communities. As a result, savings are increasingly becoming an integral component of Catholic Relief Services programming across many sectors in Central America.

Chapter 7

# Saving Cash
# and Saving the Herd

*The Role of Savings Groups
in the Livelihoods of East African Pastoralists*

Matthew Griffith

## Informal Finance on the Rangeland

From the point of view of a bank or microfinance institution, East African pastoralists are not a promising customer base. Herders in Ethiopia, Somalia, and Northern Kenya face problems of illiteracy and innumeracy, which complicate contract agreements. Most pastoralist households rely on a single strategy for food, income, and wealth storage: the raising of livestock. This critical financial asset—central to any pastoralist household's ability to meet its financial obligations—is regularly threatened by drought. Add the transaction costs of dealing with a mobile population in areas with few roads, and one can see why formal banks pay little attention to pastoralist communities.

However, where formal banks hesitate to tread, member-owned financial institutions can thrive. Informal savings groups have none of the major cost components (buildings to maintain, loan officers to pay) that deter formal institutions from reaching herders. Groups provide a savings option—a service microfinance institutions may not offer—and groups can tailor loan sizes, interest rates, procedures, and terms to the preferences of their membership. NGOs and aid agencies have noted the benefits of savings groups and now actively promote them in pastoralist areas.

However, if savings groups are poorly designed and executed, these programs can make people poorer rather than richer. Credit is, of course, debt, even if the funds are member owned. An inefficient group burdens members with heavy loans, adding to a household's financial challenges. A poorly functioning group also strains relationships by creating financial obligations among friends and neighbors. In pastoralist communities, donating cash or animals to struggling households is a critical strategy for collective survival. The erosion of social bonds resulting from new disagreements over money can weaken a centuries-old livelihood practice.

This chapter draws upon insights from a recent study on the role of savings groups in pastoralist areas. Currently, broad trends such as population growth and global warming are making traditional pastoralist livelihood strategies less successful. The study found that, with some communities, promoted savings groups were indeed bolstering social and financial well-being. In others, inappropriate implementation practices were straining an already difficult situation. Successful interventions begin with a fundamental respect for the livelihood challenges of the rangeland, an ecology that has rejected both sedentary ranching and all but a few isolated patches of cultivation. By advocating the rewards of savings groups without an honest emphasis on the risks, promoting agencies can undermine those they seek to help.

## Pastoralist Livelihoods and the Financial Damage of Drought

The East African rangeland follows seasonal rainfall patterns. In good years the rains arrive as expected, sufficient in both duration and volume to replenish supplies of fodder and water. In bad years the rains are light or nonexistent, the region faces drought, and the all-important herds are endangered.

The all-importance of the herd is foremost a matter of household diet. Most of the calories people eat in these areas come from milk, meat, and blood, derived directly from the family's herd.[1] While pastoralists are increasingly taking up different ways of earning money, livestock sales still make up the bulk of household cash income, between 60 and 85 percent by some estimates.[2] Without access to financial services, extra cash is reinvested in the herd as the safest and most productive way to store wealth. Increasing market integration has opened up possibilities for wage labor, petty trading of goods, and better livestock marketing. However, most pastoralists are still livestock producers, closely watching the skies for the rain clouds that indirectly keep the family fed.

In the language of the Dikicha people of southern Ethiopia, the word for drought is *Olla-Bukuti*, meaning "an unmerciful and selfish situation, whereby every life is at the verge of death."[3] The words convey the destruction that drought causes. Drought is a livelihoods contagion, spreading from the rangeland to the animals to the household. Insufficient rains deplete water and vegetation resources. Animals that survive the drought period are emaciated and weak. Unhealthy animals cease to produce milk and are more likely to catch and spread disease.

As the nutritional yield from the herd falls, a family must increasingly feed itself with grain. But grain is purchased at the market, and during a drought the terms of trade do not favor livestock producers. Emaciated animals are worth less than healthy animals, and the prices pastoralists receive fall. Additionally, since drought affects everyone in the region, all producer households are looking to sell at the same time. Supply in the livestock market increases, pushing livestock prices down again.[4] At the same time, and for the same reasons, the demand for grain is rising, pushing grain prices up. Commanding lower prices for their animals and facing higher prices for grain, household finances are squeezed from both sides.

Drought is damaging, but it is not new, and East African pastoralists have many traditional coping strategies. The most important are the basic tenets of the pastoralist system: seasonal herd movement in order to access year-round water sources and allow local fodder vegetation to recover; and collective resource management by traditional leaders and institutions. Additionally, households accumulate animals as a financial buffer against times of strain, diversify livestock species and breeds to protect against disease, diversify sources of income (such as having some members work as casual wage laborers), and draw upon other households in the reciprocal systems of social insurance mentioned earlier.

Using strategies such as these, pastoralism perseveres in an ecology that has proven inhospitable to all other livelihood systems. However, global warming means drought is occurring more frequently, resulting in less time for pastoralists to rebuild their herds before the next drought hits.[5] More frequent droughts, combined with population growth and controversial government policies that cut off access to dry-season resources such as springs and rivers, are making traditional coping mechanisms less effective and increasingly insufficient.

## The Study

Pastoralists have always engaged in trade, but in the last twenty-five years the use of physical cash has increased significantly. Pastoralist households now seek wage employment, petty trading opportunities, and more profitable ways to market and sell their livestock. More market activity increases the need for effective financial management. With formal financial institutions huddled in commercial centers, member-owned savings groups have emerged as a promising way to increase access to financial services.

Thus, as part of a USAID-funded project called the Pastoralist Livelihoods Initiative, several international aid agencies partnered with local NGOs to help households keep fed and healthy through the drought cycle without having to liquidate a dangerously large portion of their animals. The project included veterinary care, rangeland management training, improved access to water resources, and early warning alerts of drought. And it included a bit of money to promote savings groups.

In the summer of 2008, with a research grant from the Feinstein International Center at Tufts University, we conducted a short, qualitative assessment of groups promoted by an international NGO and its local partners. The author was the lead researcher, aided generously by NGO workers in various regions. Focusing on the Borana region in the south and the Afar region in the northeast of the country, we met leaders and rank-and-file members from fifteen groups, including twelve-member women's savings groups, sixty-member women's cooperatives, and male-headed livestock marketing cooperatives of various sizes. We also interviewed livelihood officers on the ground, project directors at agency headquarters, and academics in the national capital, Addis Ababa. Following is a short discussion of our findings.

## Modest Gains and Success in Business

In general, the groups that participated in the study were ASCAs, generating cash from member savings, eventually accumulating enough for internal lending. Unsurprisingly, we found that the consistent first use of either savings or credit was the purchase of livestock. The most commonly cited benefit of access to credit was the ability to buy a young goat, fatten it, sell it for a profit, and repay the loan. Some of the groups had purchased livestock collectively, allowing for the acquisition of far larger and more lucrative animals, such as those displayed in a village in the Afar region. Behind an impenetrable arrangement of stick and barb sat seven well-fed and well-shaded cows—the primary investment of an organized and disciplined livestock-marketing group.

The groups also provided modest financial security against drought. Outside of groups, pastoralist households usually store their wealth in the form of animals—camels and cattle rather than bills and coins. If a producer household has no cash when a drought hits, it faces the double squeeze—reduced income from livestock sales, and increased expenditure for buying grain. Membership in a savings group can provide access to cash without having to sell an animal. Several group members described taking out a loan to buy grain during a drought, and using that money to cover the caloric shortfall of the hardest period. They could then wait out the drought period when livestock prices were low, sell their animals for better prices after the drought had passed, and repay the loan.

As groups acquired more skills and experience, they often took on more complicated financial operations. Many of the female-headed groups with whom we spoke had moved into petty trading of goods, building on NGO-provided training and their own entrepreneurial ambitions to gain the necessary skills. These groups explained that few people in their villages enjoyed trekking half a day or more to pick up basic necessities, like soap, sugar, and tea. If these goods were available locally, they could be sold at a premium.

One women's group ran an impressive petty-trading enterprise beside the main highway between Addis Ababa and Djibouti sea ports. While we were present, members of local communities and passing truckers ambled up to the modest mud-wall and corrugated-iron-roof structure to buy basic goods. This advantageous location, within reach of two modest-sized towns, made restocking the shelves convenient and cheap. Business was so good that the group had purchased a refrigerator, so it could make better profits by selling cold water and soft drinks.

The women who owned this shop were clear and consistent. The group had straightforward rules governing savings, lending, and interest, which they called a service charge in this predominantly Muslim region, in deference to the Islamic prohibition on usury. Internal-lending requests were considered collectively. If a member's request was approved, she received a fixed loan of thirty dollars, due in three months along with a 10 percent service charge. After two years of building transparent practices and a disciplined operation, the savings group was ready to open its shop. Group savings—plus thirteen-hundred dollars in seed funding from an NGO—supplied the initial capital. The group's discipline, persistence, and savvy transformed this investment into a profitable and robust business.

## Liabilities and the Frustration of Failed Enterprise

The group members we interviewed also described how participation in the group could strain and damage their livelihoods. Regular savings are an additional financial obligation; regular meetings take additional time. Members described how, during times of drought, women might make round trips of twenty-five kilometers or more to retrieve water. Given such demands on their time, they reported, an afternoon group meeting was an additional burden that diminished group participation and enthusiasm.

Members and NGO workers on the ground repeated a similar list of negative ways that the arrival of savings-group promotion can affect a pastoralist community. Debt burdens increase individual households' financial hardship; financial disagreements cause strife, weakening important relationships and undermining traditional systems of social insurance; husbands may resent their wives' participation in women-only groups, creating conflict within the household; and new power dynamics resulting from new forms of financial success erode the traditional political institutions on which pastoralists have relied for hundreds of years.

Moreover, implementing organizations all too often push groups into complicated financial activities for which they are not prepared. For every successful group selling cold water to truckers out of its refrigerator, we encountered several that had sunk their collective funds into a failed microenterprise, one which required operation and management skills that were beyond the capacity of group members.

This problem of inappropriate pacing was especially prevalent in livestock-marketing operations. It is tempting to organize livestock producers—the pastoralist households themselves—to become more effective collective livestock marketers because such organization holds out the promise of increasing the value of pastoralists' most important assets. In theory, effective livestock-marketing groups start like any other savings group: regular member contributions lead to organized internal lending, with the members building their financial acumen all the while. Eventually, if a group decides to move into livestock marketing, it takes on the role of a community-minded trader. The group rounds up animals from local producer households and travels to the market with a larger stock than any individual would have had alone, thus reducing transaction costs and enhancing bargaining power.

However, on the ground such operations are complicated and difficult. Livestock marketing involves high initial capital requirements, transport difficulties once the animals have been collected, variable and unpredictable demand at markets, and

complicated business relationships with both professional traders and pastoralist producers. Without enough financial education and experience, livestock-marketing groups lead to financial
liabilities and social strain rather than the profits and growth the
promoting agencies envisioned.

One group with whom we spoke told us about its persistent
frustration with its livestock-marketing operations in the town of
Yabelo, near the Kenyan border. The group was well placed,
serving producer communities near two major towns, one of
which had a weekly livestock market with well-kept facilities.
However, the philosophy of the local implementing NGO was to
start all groups as cooperatives—a government-recognized financial entity that was far larger than an informal savings group.
The group began with fifty members drawn from a wide geographical region that included several ethnic groups. This het-
erogeneity and geographic dispersion made trust and transparency
difficult, because the members were both physically and cultur-
ally distant from one another.

Further, the group skipped the critical period of internal savings and lending, going instead directly into its joint marketing
business. The group collected an initial buy-in contribution of
twenty-six dollars from each member, amounting to over one
thousand dollars of member-generated capital. But there was no
regular savings requirement. Instead, the groups used an immediate two thousand dollar grant from the NGO as seed capital, a
well-intentioned contribution that too often erodes group financial discipline and self-reliance.

With its cash in hand, the group started its livestock-marketing enterprise, but with very little success. Grim faces looked
downward as the leaders described how the entire group had
only made six hundred dollars in profits in two years. Even their
three thousand dollars in member savings and NGO seed capital
seemed impotent in comparison to the twenty or thirty thousand
dollars wielded by professional livestock traders. They told us
that the training had been insufficient and was soon disregarded,
and the absence of alternatives kept the operation locked into
the weekly livestock market, which reduced the group's bargaining power. The leaders felt that the outlook for their group
was not good, and they openly wondered whether to continue
an enterprise for which they were so clearly unprepared.

## Conclusion: Pacing Pastoralist Savings Groups

The nature of institutional aid—from NGOs, government, or whomever—is such that many financial-development interventions disappear when the budget is cut. Thus, in pastoralist areas, it was clear that good savings-group promotion should equip members with the knowledge, skills, and experience necessary to maintain operations without external support. Thorough financial education is difficult and slow in any context. In pastoralist regions the task is complicated by extremely low rates of literacy and numeracy and by people's lack of experience with cash-based savings or credit. We found some implementing organizations that understood these challenges and were supporting profitable if modest groups. We also discovered some that did not and were promoting groups that were visibly frustrated and concerned about their financial future.

Promoting organizations must tailor and pace their support to the financial goals of the group. In difficult pastoralist regions they should err on the side of restraint. More complicated operations—such as livestock marketing and petty trading—can indeed yield large returns. However, group members and NGO workers told us that groups which take on too much too quickly are the least effective and the most burdensome to their members. It is generally far better to establish an efficient and self-reliant savings group with modest financial gains for its members than to push groups into complex financial operations prematurely.

We found no standard time frame along which groups should progress. Some groups enjoyed more effective leadership, easier access to a market center, or other advantages that allowed them to undertake more complicated financial enterprises more rapidly. The critical consideration was not how much time had passed but whether the group had achieved effective financial practices, such as consistent attendance at meetings, good record keeping, a history of successful internal lending and repayment, and general satisfaction as reported by the rank-and-file members.

Pastoral people have successfully adapted to ecological constraints that consistently discourage all other livelihood systems.

However, a changing world is making it more difficult for their systems to be economically viable. Financial development can expand the economic entitlement of pastoralists, but the constraints and transaction costs of doing business in pastoralist regions keep formal financial institutions in the cities and commercial centers.

Member-owned savings groups sidestep many of these constraints and can thus be an effective development approach. However, ill-adapted programming—specifically regarding the issue of pacing—can undermine pastoralist livelihood outcomes rather than bolster them. The potential for positive impact exists, so long as promoting agencies sufficiently respect the livelihood challenges of the rangeland.

## Notes

[1] Elliot Fratkin, "East African Pastoralism in Transition: Massai, Boran, and Rendille Cases," *African Studies Review* 44 no. 3 (2001): 1–25.

[2] Ced Hesse and James MacGregor, "Pastoralism: 'Drylands' Invisible Asset? Developing a Framework for Assessing the Value of Pastoralism in East Africa," IIED issue paper no. 142 (2006): 17.

[3] Fassil Kebebew, Diress Tsegaye, and Gry Synnevag, "Traditional Coping Strategies of the Afar and Borana Pastoralists in Response to Drought," Drylands Coordination Group Report no. 17 (2001): 13.

[4] Fratkin, "East African Pastoralism in Transition," 8.

[5] Christian Aid, *Life on the Edge of Climate Change: The Plight of Pastoralists in Northern Kenya* (London: Christian Aid, 2003), 8.

Chapter 8

# Informal Group-Based Savings Services

## The Indian Experience

GIRIJA SRINIVASAN AND N. SRINIVASAN

## Introduction

Stuart Rutherford, in several of his writings, has underlined the importance of savings services for the poor.[1] Households living on limited financial resources want services that allow them to capture small surpluses when they arise, and to protect those surpluses from evaporating in the face of daily consumption. The poorer the people, the more critical is their need for savings.

Mechanisms that effectively convert the surpluses of the poor into savings are characterized by (1) local availability, (2) ability to motivate the poor to part with their meager surpluses, (3) ability to make cash available in times of emergency, and (4) sufficient accessibility to the illiterate and semiliterate. If the funds remain within the local area, savers feel confident that they will have access to those funds in times of need.

Historically, people have saved their surplus wealth in the form of money, grain, cattle, gold, and the like. These assets might go out as loans to others, creating a resource that is available to be recalled during times of need. These informal strategies do their part, but they do come with large risks. Many physical assets decline in value over time. Without clear accounting practices and agreements, people often lose their money. With informal financial arrangements there is rarely any formal record of amounts saved or any stipulation of the time frame after which savings can be recalled. Further, there is often no return on the savings, and the physical safety of the funds is not assured.

In India, informal savings systems have a long history. ROSCAs, ASCAs, thrift-and-credit groups, chit funds, grain banks, funeral associations, and other informal arrangements have existed in different contexts and served a variety of financial purposes. India's self-help groups (SHGs), which cover more than seventy million households, have been an important innovation in the provision of savings services to the poor and marginalized. This innovation is the focus of this article.

## A Brief History

Group-based savings intermediation became popular in India in the mid 1990s, and has since grown exponentially. This growth was driven by a supportive policy environment and a healthy volunteer ethic among NGOs. Additionally, the Indian banking system was interested in the potential of this new market, and India's apex development bank—the National Bank for Agriculture and Rural Development (NABARD)—was willing to foster the SHG idea and to catalyze the growth of the program. NABARD piloted formation of the first groups, set the policies governing linkages with formal banks, provided training, funded pilot programs, and provided capital to the banks that could then be lent for agriculture and microfinance.

NABARD funded a well-known NGO, MYRADA, to form the first several hundred groups through known and respected Indian NGOs. What started as a very small pilot in the late 1980s today includes a few million groups and over seventy million households. By March 2007, about two thousand NGOs were forming groups and linking them with banks. Early on, these savings groups grew most vigorously in the southern part of India, but after 2005 they were rapidly appearing in eastern and western regions of India as well.

In terms of numbers this SHG and bank linkage program is the largest group-based microfinance program in the world, uniting tens of millions of participants under a single, simple concept: genuine decentralization. This concept—one of the program's most unique and defining features—involves NGOs and government departments working in collaboration with banks, leading to the emergence of context-specific models and best practices.

## How Do Informal Groups Help the Poor to Save?

Group formation is typically facilitated by an NGO, which helps groups of ten to twenty individuals with homogeneous backgrounds—such as similar cultural, ethnic, and financial status—cluster into groups. More recently, government staff, bank officials, schoolteachers, community health workers, and others have engaged in group formation as well.

Over a series of initial meetings each new group adopts a set of rules governing its internal functioning. Groups decide the frequency of their meetings and the amount that they will save every week, or every two weeks, or every month, according to their convenience and ability. The amount of savings is the same for all members. Most members are illiterate or semiliterate, and a fixed savings rate makes accounting easy. Moreover, members' eligibility for a bank loan is linked to their amount of savings, and the members prefer to keep loan eligibility fairly uniform within the group to avoid the risk of a few wealthier individuals monopolizing the loans. Group rules require the members to attend all meetings, save regularly, observe loan-related discipline, and take part in any joint activities of the group. The emphasis on discipline is to ensure that the members save regularly, borrow according to need and repayment capacity, and keep up payments on existing loans.

Group members contribute their time to attend meetings, where they carry out transactions and update and maintain their accounts. Their willingness to conduct these operations themselves, rather than hire an outside financial professional, is a critical way of keeping group costs down.

Members use group savings as capital for internal loans; surplus funds not used for loans go into a bank account. After six to twelve months of independent operation—if the group has displayed consistently high-quality performance—groups gain access to bank loans as an additional source of internal-lending capital. Group members track each other's repayment performance. Friends and neighbors doubling as financial partners provide both support and pressure, ensuring continued regular savings and loan repayment.

While most groups offer interest on members' savings—usually between 7 and 8 percent[2]—some do not. Members share equally any interest income they pay on their individual loans from the group fund by depositing the interest into their collective "savings pot," which then becomes available to go out again in loans. The interest they earn by on-lending bank loans to members likewise goes into the collective group fund.

However, individual members are not permitted to withdraw their money on demand. This restriction does not mean members never enjoy the fruits of their discipline. The group as a whole might decide, perhaps once in a few years, to divide and disburse the accumulated funds among members. In some older groups, where the procedures are tight and discipline unbending, that disbursal might happen only after seven to ten years. In such cases members might receive between $550 and $750 at share-out. This is the equivalent of about two years' income for some households and is often sufficient to replace a roof, buy a healthy cow, or invest in some other critical livelihood asset.

Compared to average per capita savings of $366 in India as a whole,[3] the $53 savings per capita figure in mature SHGs[4] may seem low. However, many SHG members had no regular cash savings until they joined the group. For the first time in their lives, group members have their own savings, and these savings grow by substantial amounts year after year. More important, these savings give members access to loans from within their own groups and from banks. Loan capital from banks can amount to up to ten times members' cumulative savings, thus providing a large enough source of capital to meet the credit needs of group members. And one must not forget the central point and benefit of these self-owned financial institutions: all loans made by the group, including those made with their own internal savings and with bank loans, generate interest for the group which is divided and added to members' accounts, increasing overall savings.

## Savings Performance

As of March 2009, 5.9 million groups had saved an estimated $118 million in banks, in addition to internal group funds that had not been deposited. Eighty percent of these groups, totaling 4.72 million SHGs, were composed only of women. A number of agencies studying SHGs estimated the annual savings of India's 4.1 million groups to be about $1.3 billion in March 2007.[5] At that time, groups' internal funds were estimated to amount to about $2.8 billion.

Table 8–1. Total Savings of SHGs in Banks, March 31, 2009

| Name of the Agency | No. of SHGs | Amount of Savings (millions of dollars) | Average Amount of Savings per SHG (dollars) |
|---|---|---|---|
| Commercial Banks | 3,549,509 | 602.8 | 170 |
| Regional Rural Banks | 1,556,608 | 419.6 | 270 |
| Co-operative Banks | 882,902 | 161.7 | 183 |
| **Total** | **5,989,019** | **1184.1** | **198** |

NABARD, *Status of Microfinance in India 2008–09* (Mumbai, India: NABARD, 2009).

SHGs account for about 9 percent of all savings accounts maintained with all forms of financial institutions in India. When the multiplicity of accounts maintained by the same individual with banks is reckoned, the number of clients accessing savings services through groups could be more than 15 percent of all Indian savers.

## Are Self-help Groups the Best Solution for Financial Inclusion?

SHGs and their promoters do not claim that groups offer savings services that equal those from banks. Instead, these groups provide a simple and specialized service—fixed savings

### Table 8–2. SHGs Compared to Other Types of Savings Accounts in India, March 31, 2009

| Institution | Number of Deposit Accounts (millions) |
|---|---|
| Commercial Banks | 320.9 |
| Regional Rural Banks | 52.7 |
| Urban Cooperative Banks | 50 |
| Post Office | 60.8 |
| Primary Cooperative Societies | 60 |
| Self-help Groups (member savers) | 53.3 |
| **Total** | **597.7** |

Data on commercial banks and regional rural banks reported are from the Reserve Bank of India's website (www.rbi.org.in). According to the National Federation of State Cooperative Banks (www.nafscob.org), primary cooperatives have a membership of 120 million. In the absence of relevant data, 50 percent of members are assumed to have savings accounts with their societies. Data on SHGs are from NABARD, *Status of Microfinance in India 2008–09* (Mumbai, India: NABARD, 2009).

at periodic intervals—that helps the poor manage their limited financial resources.

One of the greatest strengths of SHGs is that they provide a path of financial education and experience that often leads people to formal institutions. Groups set the amount of their fixed periodic savings, and that amount stays the same every period unless the entire group decides to change it. The savings contribution is compulsory and cannot exceed the amount set by the group. Members who want to save more than the fixed amount must find other places to do so. Once they have gained some familiarity with formal financial institutions through their group's link to a bank, members who would like to save more sometimes save directly with banks. Being members of the group enables them to comply with "know your client" regulations, a body of rules that are designed to protect both clients and financial institutions from excessive debt or suspicious activity. Banks are familiar with group members through the interactions they have with them while providing loans to the group. Anecdotal evidence suggests that nearly one-third of members eventually open individual savings accounts with banks.

The fact that with groups, savings are tied up for long periods of time, during which savers cannot withdraw their money on demand, is indeed a limitation. If a group member wants her savings back, the entire group must decide whether all or part of her savings can be returned to her. The decision affects everyone, since it has implications for the continued availability and size of loans that the group can access from banks. When making a loan to a group, banks consider the group's volume of savings and fix the loan size as a multiple of this. If the group's savings are drawn down, banks scale down their loan limits.

Many people have expressed reservations about the involuntary nature of savings in SHGs. But there are fundamental advantages to compulsory savings, and even formal financial institutions serving more affluent people sometimes use such restrictions. Pension and annuity plans require recurring contributions during the accumulation phase, money that can only be recovered after retirement. Many retirement plans are not available for use before a pre-established age. In the case of the poor, inflexible group savings can be a useful tool for encouraging self-discipline, helping members resist the temptation to spend all income on daily needs and wants.

Avoiding voluntary withdrawals also frees SHGs from having to manage day-to-day liquidity, which would require constant adjustments to internal records and accounts. The more complicated management and accounting required for voluntary withdrawals pose operational risks. The groups are disinclined to allow withdrawal of savings on demand because this can place members' savings at risk. At group meetings, members in need of quick cash are allowed to take loans. While they pay interest on those loans, the interest they pay eventually goes back into their group's account.

Group members do face the risk of losing their savings when borrowing members default. Since savings are lent within the groups, the risk of default is minimal. Members know that part of their savings is lent out, and they ensure that repayment rates are maintained, applying sufficient pressure on the given borrower as needed. Further, members' loan requests are negotiated during group meetings, and the most urgent needs are prioritized. In setting the terms of loans, members' intimate knowledge of one another helps considerably.

While default has historically been low, the risk is rising. The exponential growth in the numbers of groups has expanded membership to include some "sub-prime" members, individuals who do not have the discipline to meet their obligations. Additionally, some facilitating NGOs and lending banks have employed weak information systems, making it difficult to manage their portfolios effectively and to anticipate and address challenges. Members can also take steps to protect their savings, for example, by depositing cash surpluses in formal insured bank accounts, where their funds are protected from loss.

Given the efficiency and low cost with which millions of people have formed groups and started saving, the SHG model is an ideal tool to bring about more formal financial inclusion. In order to establish relationships with new customers, banks must be able to service their accounts. While such servicing is very difficult for banks to do independently, particularly in remote areas, SHGs can reduce these costs by facilitating easier access to poor customers. Banks have embraced this opportunity for increasing financial inclusion, as evidenced by the recent trend of banks hiring NGOs as correspondents to finance groups. In the correspondent model a bank hires an NGO on a commission basis to acquire clients and process financial transactions on behalf of the bank. HDFC Bank exclusively services SHG clients through this arrangement; it had 41,680 of them by March 2009.

## Current Operational Challenges and Debates

In addition to the limitations of the SHG mechanism itself, operational and strategic problems pose other challenges. These focus largely on the most effective and sustainable methods for forming and supporting new groups.

The cost of creating groups is high, because the initial training and support period is both long and intense. The cost of forming and stabilizing a group has been computed by NCAER to be in the range of $75 to $180, depending on the agency involved.[6] While donors, banks, and governments fund the formation and linking of groups, this money does not always cover the full costs. Group formation must be seen as an investment in infrastructure and publicly funded as such. One solution involves an innovative partnership in which banks hire NGOs to create and strengthen groups, thus covering some of the previously uncovered group start-up costs. Forming quality groups will become easier as this practice grows.

Groups formed in response to government programs have at times been of dubious quality. Groups that receive external grants and loans—rather than building their own capital and experience with their own savings—do not become strong savings groups. Even in terms of purely managing credit, their performance has not been very good. It is important for government and other donors who invest in group formation to develop a shared understanding of the fundamental principles of SHGs, so that all groups enjoy the appropriate values and discipline that result in a robust and profitable savings group.

In the recent past there has been a move toward federating groups into broad umbrella structures, which might be able to command more resources and provide more extensive support to individual groups on the ground. Such federations can be effective if they arise in response to the needs expressed by the groups rather than being externally imposed by facilitating NGOs and others. However, federations that take up financial intermediation sometimes erode the autonomy of groups by pooling their savings and investing them according to priorities determined at higher levels. Federations that do not enjoy the support of constituent groups are a drag on the groups and contribute only to increased operation costs.

In addition to the challenges of forming and sustaining new groups, another challenge is to ensure adequate access to bank linkages over the long term. The phenomenal increase in group numbers seems to have caused some fatigue within the formal financial-services industry, and some groups are reporting that banks are reluctant to do business with them.

## Conclusion

Group-based savings intermediation helps the poor access needed financial services within their own communities. Linkages allow banks to service a more diverse client base without having to open large numbers of individual accounts with small balances. Groups also help the government deliver development services more efficiently by providing an organized entry point into communities. Overall, SHGs create a win-win situation for all stakeholders. The quality of financial services and the variety offered may not be the best possible, but groups amount to an effective alternative to formal banking, one that adequately serves the needs of the poor.

In the search for an ideal savings product for the poor, the aspiration of perfection should not hinder the expansion and evolution of a good and useful model. The group-based saving services of SHGs in India and elsewhere should move forward as a very simple, low-cost solution to meet the most pressing financial-services needs of the poor.

## Notes

[1] Stuart Rutherford, *The Poor and Their Money: An Essay about Financial Services for Poor People* (New Delhi, India: Oxford University Press, 2000).

[2] NCAER (National Council of Applied Economic Research), *Impact and Sustainability of SHG Bank Linkage Program* (New Delhi, India: NCAER, 2008).

[3] Reserve Bank of India, "Basic Statistical Returns of Scheduled Commercial Banks in India," *RBI* 36 (2007).

[4] NCAER, *Impact and Sustainability of SHG Bank Linkage Program*, 2008.

[5] Ibid.

[6] Ibid.

Malian group leaders track deposits and loan payments in full
view of group membership.

# PART 3

# MORE WAYS OF SKINNING THE CAT, AND DIFFERENT KINDS OF CATS

It is in the nature of "experts" and other outsiders to classify the infinite variety of human activities into different types, and to label them, often with bewildering acronyms—ROSCAs, ASCAs, and SHGs can be promoted by MFIs or NGOs. . . . But these terms should not delude us into believing that real-world phenomena can actually be put into neat boxes. There are as many different kinds of groups as there are different types of people and situations, and one of the main strengths of voluntary savings groups is that their members can design and manage them to suit local needs.

In Kenya, mobile telephones are becoming a preferred tool for financial transactions, even among the poor. In Chapter 9 Kim Wilson tells the story of Jipange Sasa and how this new technology is being used to facilitate group savings in Kibera, a large slum in Nairobi. Groups, under the inspiration of a powerful community organizer, have devised ingenious ways to forward savings to their communal fund, and in so doing have cut down on risky and valuable travel time to and from meetings.

Financial services are not the only entry point for development institutions interested in promoting savings groups. Savings and lending can be appropriate adjuncts to other interventions in areas like health, sanitation, or agricultural extension. In Chapter 10, for example, Vinod Parmeshwar and Yang Saing Koma describe how Oxfam applied new savings practices to previously formed farmers' clubs. Their efforts have met with partial success and have demonstrated several key lessons. Their chapter demonstrates how difficult it is to pour new wine into old bottles.

CARE has long experience in applying corporate-management methods to development programs. In Chapter 11 Anthony Murathi, Nelly Otieno, and Paul Rippey show how CARE is experimenting with individual entrepreneurs and church-based institutions as distribution channels for group formation in Kenya, in order to reduce the cost per member without diluting group quality.

Julie Zollmann and Guy Vanmeenen describe in Chapter 12 ways in which other NGOs are applying mass marketing techniques to the promotion of savings groups. CARE, Catholic Relief Services, Pact, and Plan are all experimenting with outsourcing the establishment and development of groups to local promoters through multilevel franchisees, in order to reduce the cost and enhance the sustainability of the promotion process.

A powerful series of workshops held in 2008 inspired community volunteerism and the growth of the thousands of savings groups now flourishing in Haiti's hard-pressed southern peninsula. Kim Wilson and Gaye Burpee describe in Chapter 13 one program, run from a local church organization, that is representative of many other rapidly expanding savings-group efforts. Through this program three part-time workers, operating without the usual artifacts of development—manuals, forms, tool kits— were able to create more than seven hundred groups.

Commercial banks usually find it uneconomic to offer savings facilities which are suitable for poor people. The individual deposits and withdrawals and account balances are too small. Physical and social distance and other constraints also mean that clients' transaction costs are too high. In the final chapter of this section, Wajiha Ahmed describes how the First Microfinance Bank, a Pakistani financial-services provider, is promoting groups solely for savings mobilization, with no necessary link to a loan.

Chapter 9

# Jipange Sasa

*A Little Heaven of Local Savings, Hot Technologies,*
*and Formal Finance*

KIM WILSON

## Kibera

A slum city located entirely within the Kenyan capital of Nairobi, Kibera is home to more than a million people. It is a place with no public systems of toilets, roads, schools, or sewage. It has no police. Residents must purchase the water they drink.

In the rainy season its dirt roads dissolve into brown glue and stall the commute of residents in and out of the slum. In the dry season its roads harden and buckle, redirecting the course of the sullage that sometimes passes for water in Kibera. In the violent season, during political elections, its roads lead desperate families out of the slum and into hiding up-country.

Imagine yourself in Kibera. As you plod along its lanes, edged by a cookie dough of soil and human waste, taking in the rot of the streets, breathing its decay, you might not dare to imagine that a few of the people here are beginning to hoist themselves out of this dreary situation. But that is exactly what is happening.

The man making this possible is Lukas Alube—educator, firebrand, and financial engineer. He has spliced together a grid of real and virtual money served up by the market, the hottest technologies available, and unstinting volunteerism.

The result: Those who were once considered some of the poorest residents of Kibera now save regularly, self-insure against the death of a family member, and invest in securities through the Nairobi Stock Exchange. This fresh breed of investor is able to fund his or her daily consumption of food and water, set aside money for household emergencies, and plan—against all odds but, as we shall learn, not against all hope—for a future beyond Kibera.

This chapter is about how savings groups start slowly, growing out of local savings and burial practices. When trust among members is firm, groups evolve into Village Savings and Lending Associations (VSLAs). As money circulates within the associations, members begin to improve the efficiency of their financial self-service. With the help of Jipange Sasa, the organization formed by Alube, associations graft their simple practices onto a telecommunications and banking platform unique to Kenya. The resulting hybrid delivers speedy record keeping and depositing, enables increased savings balances, and facilitates group investment in the Kenyan stock market.

## The Ministry of Finance

Alube was born in Kibera and recalls his high school days playing football on its once expansive fields. He was able to move out of the slum twelve years ago, returning daily to visit friends, relatives, and new residents. These days Alube spends his time picking his way along the rough paths of Kibera to dispense ideas, scold pessimists, and encourage all who will listen that they can, if they work together, find ways to leave behind Kibera and their poverty.

Trained in community finance by the Chalmers Center of Economic Development at Covenant College in the United States, Alube came across the work of Hugh Allen—an early pioneer in village savings and lending—during a workshop sponsored by the Anglican community. Allen's model instantly caught the activist's attention. "The approach was so relevant," Alube remembers. "At last I had a practical way to help people stuck in their routines of daily survival."

He tried his hand at forming savings groups. They worked. Emboldened, Alube launched Jipange Sasa ("plan now") in 2004. Jipange Sasa is a small, voluntary organization that helps people wrest savings from their meager livings so that they can one day leave Kibera. As Alube puts it, "This is not a place that you work to improve. People here must get out, and for that they must fight." Savings is part of the fight. So are savings groups. Alube manages fifteen such groups but has coaxed many more into existence. His world is one of "paying it forward." Groups thank him for his time by forming other groups.

Jipange Sasa spreads its financial gospel in several ways; its volunteers form new groups but also teach existing self-help clubs, abundant in Kibera, to add savings and lending to their missions. Originally, these clubs sprang to life from a call to civic work. Club members collected and disposed of trash, policed the local neighborhood, and cared for children. By adding savings-and-loan services to their activities, self-help clubs acquired more financial resources to invest in their social work.

"In my own groups," Alube says, "the ones I begin from scratch, I have had to start very simply. With 'dear ones' [his term for the poorest of the poor] I must begin at the beginning. I work with what they know, where they are, and what they fear. These members are often new to Kibera, are out of money, frightened, and a little desperate."

Alube starts his dear ones off with a merry-go-round, a kind of savings club pervasive throughout rural Kenya. The rules of a merry-go-round seem familiar, and therefore safe, to dear ones. Ten or twenty members gather into a club. Each member contributes the same sum of money every week, and every week one member takes the whole sum home. Over time, each member has a turn at receiving the lump sum.

After a merry-go-round is up and running, Alube begins to address what his dear ones fear most—death. Custom dictates that the residents of Kibera observe the rituals of village burial: "They worry about living so far away from home and about the enormous costs of a proper ceremony. How will they ever come up with the amount they need? And they also worry about what their spouses and children will do if they die."

He encourages members to start a burial fund, with each member contributing the same sum every month, from ten to fifty shillings (about \$0.13 to \$0.16), depending on the amount which the group has decided. Funds are deposited in a bank. The burial fund is not touched until a group member dies, in which case the spouse or child of the member receives a fixed amount of money—never enough to cover the full costs of a funeral, but always enough to begin preparations.

Drawing on these two basic services—the merry-go-round method of savings and the burial fund method of insurance—Alube helps the groups to make their practices more sophisticated. He advises them to allow a portion of their savings to accumulate, and he shows them how to lend this new pool of funds to members.

Members borrow to fund emergencies, to purchase drinking water and food, or to travel to and from Kibera. Once everyone trusts one another and the system, Alube encourages them to develop joint businesses. Members enjoy the confidence gained by working shoulder to shoulder with others in the same situation. Together members sell vegetables, run a *matatu* (taxi) service, or vend shoes and clothing. The most profitable business, Alube says, is to install a tap and supply water to neighbors for a fee.

During the process of coaching groups, Alube gives out financial advice: avoid local microfinance institutions ("interest rates are exorbitant"); reject get-rich-quick offers ("scams are everywhere"); and save every single day ("even five shillings makes a difference"). He also teaches members to plan and to save for a reason ("without a reason, a saver is a miser").

## The Technology of Transfer

Daily deposits, a cornerstone of Jipange Sasa's teachings, are difficult for members to make. The solution? Integrate a human web of local deposit-collectors into a mobile-phone-based cash-transfer system. But before we get to that, let us back up a bit to learn what happens in the absence of such a solution.

Normally, many small expenses—from drinking alcohol to mobile texting—gobble up what little cash a household might save. To shield money from temptation, savers must make a constant effort to move cash out of their pocket and into a safe place. The group fund is that safe place. But in normal circumstances, making frequent deposits is nearly impossible.

Members reside in Kibera but earn their living far from where groups meet. Members can spend hours on public transport traveling to and from their livelihoods. Many work in the evenings as guards or in other night-shift jobs scattered throughout Nairobi. For these members, attending weekly meetings is out of the question. But letting cash lie idle or close at hand for a month eliminates the chance of pooling it into savings.

Despite hardship, most group members are able to put between ten and fifty cents a day into the fund. Some cannot save every day but can do so weekly. How do they manage this?

Jipange Sasa has knit together its far-flung savers into an ingenious network of group deposit collectors and cash-transfer agents. Deposit collectors are unpaid members of a savings group who volunteer their services for the good of their fellow members. For example, a group of fifty members might have five subgroups, each with a designated collector located close to its membership. Collectors, daily or weekly, seek out members to take in cash savings.

Next, deposit collectors use their mobile phones to forward cash through a mobile transfer service, called M-PESA, to the group account. The account is managed by an elected treasurer. Commercially launched in 2007 by Safaricom (Kenya's largest mobile-network operator), M-PESA allows customers to make cash transfers using their Safaricom service. A network of fourteen thousand authorized agents across Kenya forms the retail backbone of M-PESA. Customers visit an agent—there are forty agents in Kibera alone—to deposit cash, which the agent turns into stored value in their M-PESA accounts. For many, M-PESA has become a savings account. Customers can transfer the cash to relatives or creditors, but they can also keep a balance in their account and withdraw money as they wish. M-PESA charges no fee for deposits and about $0.33 for each transfer or withdrawal.

M-PESA is useful to individual customers at any income level, but it is of particular use to savings groups. Working through a designated deposit collector, groups build up their funds each week. For example, if a group agrees that members will save ten shillings a day each (about $0.12), and the collector is responsible for the deposits of five members, by nightfall the collector is able to collect and deposit fifty shillings into his M-PESA account. Weekly, for a fee of $0.33, the collector forwards the $3.00 cash from his personal account to the group account by using the "send money" feature on his phone.

In this instance, the subgroup is willing to spend 11 percent of its funds on forwarding cash. Alube says the tradeoff is worth it. First, members can move the money out of their pockets, and second, they can do so without the cost of a long commute. If members save more, the cost of cash transfers decreases in relation to savings, since M-PESA charges a flat twenty-five shilling rate for small transactions.

To withdraw cash in preparation for the meeting, the group management committee visits an M-PESA agent; each committee member punches in a PIN that only he or she knows. Groups withdraw money from their joint account once a month to satisfy member requests for new loans. Borrowers in the group make loan payments in the same way, forwarding payments through their phone to the group account.

## Time Is Money

Many benefits—let us call them bonuses—have grown from the new financial web patched together by Jipange Sasa.

Bonus one: Members save time. Members no longer need to make regular visits to the treasurer to rid themselves of cash, lest that cash be frittered away. In the past a member had to bring money physically to the treasurer to keep it safe, and coordinating those visits with other obligations was difficult. Now, by handing cash to the local deposit collector, who in turn forwards it to the group account, a member is able to deposit more frequently at lower commuting cost.

Bonus two: Increased savings in time translates into increased savings in money. Says Alube, "We have more people saving more often, which means more saving is taking place in a month." Under the old system, when collections took place at monthly meetings or during visits to the treasurer, regular savings was a challenge. Many enticements parted savers from their cash as they waited days or weeks for the next group meeting.

Bonus three: Groups can predict and solve problems before they become crises. The group management committee—elected by members—meets each week to review cash collected in the communal fund via M-PESA. Prior to the creation of the collector network, the committee could track savings and payments only at group meetings. Now the committee can seek out struggling members to resolve problems before too much time has passed.

Bonus four: Groups can replace the tedium of paperwork with more engaging activities. Since the management committee now accounts for cash before meetings, groups have shifted attention away from the mind-numbing sport of record keeping to more interesting affairs like loan disbursal, neighborhood safety, and better ways to earn a living.

## Mobile Cash Means Mobile Membership

Charles Oranje, a promoter of Jipange Sasa, relates a striking example of how a system of transfer might ease the effects of geographic dispersion. He started the Gatwikera Railway Savings Club in 2004; its members meet along the train tracks that slice through Kibera and run west to Uganda. Leaning on Alube for help, Charles began his savings group with eleven members, growing it to include fifty-four members in three years. As the group expanded, it took on people of different ethnic backgrounds.

In December 2007 violence related to recent national elections erupted in Kibera. Fires destroyed whole streets, market stalls, and homes. Voters, largely divided along ethnic lines, were protesting the national elections. Suddenly, part of the slum was on the run. Without warning, several members of the Gatwikera Railway Savings Club vanished, never to return.

Inside his humble carpentry shed, Oranje recalls what happened. He clears a table of tools and wood shavings, spreads open the club record book, and points to a few names. "We can't find these people," he says. Members left without a trace when bloodshed sent shockwaves through the settlement. "We have no way to know where these people are and can't return their savings to them. It's so sad." At that time, unlike today, most members did not have cell phones or cash-transfer services.

Alube explains that with M-PESA, groups can unfurl into the far reaches of Kenya and still, if need be, offer their members the chance to retrieve their savings. "If a similar problem happened today," Alube believes, "we could reach our uprooted dear ones."

Oranje and Alube muse about the future. Technology, they agree, makes so many activities possible. Members move out of Kibera for reasons besides election-time violence. Some leave for work, to visit family, or simply to take up residence elsewhere.

Alube wants members to be free to go and still participate in their groups; at the very least they should be able to withdraw their savings. And why not? His financial improvisation draws on a telecommunications and cash-transfer system that spans all of Kenya and just recently penetrated Tanzania.

## What Goes Around Comes Around

Digital money transfers and a net of volunteer deposit collectors facilitate the movement of cash, but they tell only part of the story of savings at Jipange Sasa. Saving means sheer discipline, believes Alube. It requires regular acts of thrift on the part of members. But it also requires a forward look. As a route out of poverty, saving must include investment, the kind that comes from the same wealth-building opportunities that make rich people rich.

Groups liked the idea of the stock market, after Alube explained to them how it worked, but they were unfamiliar with how to go about investing. Alube did his research and asked for help from places like Equity Bank and Zimele Asset Management. Volunteer experts visited groups and explained investment choices.

After discussing possibilities relative to what members could afford and risk, the groups decided to purchase shares in a unit trust, a Kenyan investment vehicle similar to a mutual fund. Unit-trust managers invest in securities traded on the Nairobi Stock

Exchange. Using M-PESA, groups can forward as little as a few dollars a month to top up their unit-trust accounts.

The groups intend to cash out one day, either wholly or in part. Members hope to spend funds on long-term financial goals like a down payment on a home, on schooling, or on their retirement. These goals are not dreams but plans. For example, one of the older groups has placed more than $1,300 in a unit trust. Individual members have started developing their own investments. Weekly, they send funds into personal unit-trust accounts. Some have even purchased shares in Safaricom itself.

Long-term investments in securities balance daily savings put toward survival in Kibera. While such strategies seem smart, they are of course risky. But Alube is optimistic. "Putting money in the market is more than finance," says Alube. "It is a way we express our hope. And, we have more than hope in the market, we have faith as well. We must, because we are now part of it."

By blending the forces of the formal financial sector with a call to social good, Jipange Sasa has created a hybrid worthy of attention. The expansion of M-PESA beyond Kenya makes it possible to imagine savings groups as tiny nodes within a financial network of global reach. Members who flee sudden violence or migrate to new markets need not abandon their involvement in homespun groups. Conflict is no longer a financial centrifuge. Nor is drought or flood or any force that might split groups apart. The tethers of Jipange Sasa, ever more elastic, can keep members centered and connected.

As Alube concludes, local savings, added to the possibilities of finance through technology, are "giving dear ones a glimpse of a little heaven beyond Kibera."

Chapter 10

# Retrofitting an Agricultural Program with Savings-Led Microfinance

*The Oxfam Experience in Cambodia*

Vinod Parmeshwar and Yang Saing Koma

## The Power of Partnership

Oxfam America introduced the Saving for Change program in Cambodia with the Centre d'Etude et de Développement Agricole Cambodgien (Cambodian Center for Study and Development in Agriculture, or CEDAC) as its implementing partner in April 2005. CEDAC was already promoting agriculture in hundreds of villages in Cambodia. CEDAC felt that savings services could help farmers build financial assets, which would then help them diversify their livelihood activities. In addition to helping farmers accumulate lump sums, savings groups would offer farmers reasonably priced credit.

The center was working with approximately seven hundred savings groups with ninety-five hundred members by April 2005. However, it was interested in improving its programming by adopting Oxfam America's training curriculum and drawing on Oxfam's technical support. Oxfam shared CEDAC's vision of providing efficient, member-owned savings and credit services to the rural poor all across Cambodia. Partnership seemed like a viable means to realize that vision.

109

Unlike other projects in which new groups are freshly formed, Oxfam and CEDAC would be working together to "retrofit" existing groups with a new methodology. The new processes were not wholly consistent with the previous savings-group principles promoted by CEDAC, and the young partnership would encounter formidable challenges right from the beginning. This article describes five of the key challenges that organizers on the ground faced while transforming CEDAC's groups from their old savings practices to Saving for Change.

### Forming new groups versus retraining existing groups

In 2005 CEDAC was more interested in retraining its existing savings groups under the new methodology than was Oxfam. Oxfam was more interested in forming new groups. As a compromise, the two organizations agreed that, during the initial period (August 2005–May 2006), CEDAC would retrain all of its existing 700 groups, as well as form an additional 150 groups. Forming the new groups offered an opportunity for promoters to learn the Saving for Change system with new participants who had not already learned an alternative methodology. These same promoters could then apply those skills to the more difficult task of retrofitting existing groups with a better savings and lending model.

It soon became clear that Saving for Change offered significant advantages over CEDAC's existing system. Among other benefits, the new methodology included:

- A simplified and more transparent record-keeping system;
- A participatory approach to developing group rules and procedures using Learning Conversations, a group-building tool that draws on adult-education techniques; and
- A clearly delineated set of roles and responsibilities for members and the management committee.

Existing groups faced big challenges in changing over to the new system, having invested significant time and effort in mastering the previous system. It proved far more difficult to unlearn a certain way of record-keeping and learn another than to learn the new system without any "baggage." Forming brand-new groups became crucial in upgrading this savings program, since new groups would provide concrete examples of improved practices. New groups would inspire existing groups to change their practices for the better.

### Developing a service delivery model

An additional problem centered around the dual focus of these groups on both savings and agricultural programming. Resources were limited, and CEDAC had a natural inclination to emphasize agricultural activities, while Oxfam favored the savings component. In order to address any inadvertent bias, Oxfam and CEDAC adopted a parallel service delivery model in which field staff focused exclusively on either savings or agriculture. Promoters working with savings groups were involved only in the promotion and training of savings groups, and nothing else. Promoters working with agricultural groups were involved in agriculture activities, and nothing else. In this way CEDAC was able to work with poor farmers through a host of development interventions, and Oxfam ensured that the savings dimension of group operations received its fair share of attention.

### Building the capacity of the implementing organization

CEDAC, like many organizations on the ground, has a high rate of staff turnover. In such situations new staff must be trained quickly and systematically on the savings methodology in order to continue forming and supporting high-quality savings groups. Such training is most efficiently provided by the implementing organization itself, rather than an outside technical partner—in this case, Oxfam.

Thus, Oxfam made it a point thoroughly to train selected CEDAC staff members on the Saving for Change methodology, with a special emphasis on adult learning techniques. These techniques—which recognize that participants bring life skills and an expectation of meaningful participation—are central to the formation of democratically managed groups. By training CEDAC staff, Oxfam ensured that a cadre of individuals who were well versed in the savings-led microfinance model would remain in place after Oxfam left.

### Contending with alternative development models

Oxfam also had to contend with other donors who were funding CEDAC to form savings groups. Some of these organizations, though well meaning, were promoting ineffective savings practices. The most prominent example was "matching funds." Under a matching-funds scheme, groups receive external money to match the amount of internal group savings. The intention is twofold: to provide incentive for member savings, and to build group capital.

While the system seems simple enough, international experience using matching funds has not been good. Matching funds tend to erode the longevity of groups, as members quickly band together to get matching funds and quickly disperse once those funds have been received. Many groups simply refuse to continue saving once they reach the matched amount.

CEDAC conducted its own action research by supporting savings groups using two different approaches: one with a matching fund, and one without. When the grant that supported those groups that received matching funds was exhausted, CEDAC observed that a high percentage of those groups disbanded. The groups had formed to get the match, not for financial self-help. Matching funds were destructive. CEDAC incorporated this lesson into its own programming, and currently none of the savings groups formed by CEDAC has a matching-fund component.

### Focusing on poverty outreach

Oxfam and CEDAC found that the very poorest people were not joining the savings-group program. The upper poor, a minority of residents who were far more able to take financial risks, were participating in the program, while the very poor, the vast majority of residents, were left out. One explanation for this was that the CEDAC program began as an agricultural intervention. By definition, the landless poor were initially excluded when farmers' groups were provided with savings and lending services. Once left out, there was little opportunity for them to join a group. In addition, the poorest people often moved to distant places in search of work. This excluded them from accessing savings and credit services.

CEDAC tried to address this problem by forming special groups of the poorest people in these communities. The solution was unsustainable, as the members became frustrated and impatient, and the groups dissolved at rates far above the program average. This result is not surprising. The poorest are often on the move, in search of new and better temporary work. They cannot meet regularly. Their income tends to depend on fragile and inconsistent jobs, making regular savings contributions burdensome. CEDAC and Oxfam eventually concluded that groups must include poor and not-so-poor members. In this way members with greater or more steady incomes can help fund those with lesser and unsteady incomes. But the poorest members still find it difficult to attend meetings consistently and to make regular savings contributions.

## Conclusion

The experience of Oxfam and CEDAC in Cambodia shows how important it is to adapt program design to the local circumstances. Nearly ten thousand people—most of them engaged directly with agriculture—had an established method for saving and lending. In an effort to act on innovations in the field—specifically the emergence of a superior methodology—and deliver those innovations directly to participants, CEDAC and Oxfam decided to retrofit the entire program. The task required a specific delivery approach, extensive in-house training and capacity building, and navigation around the siren song of matching funds. The aim was to make important structural changes to improve savings and lending services and to ensure that the poorest villagers could participate. The process has required much "give and take," with many small adjustments and compromises. Both CEDAC and Oxfam believe they are delivering a better savings product to more participants, which was the basic goal all along.

# Chapter 11

# Virtual Staff

*Exploring a Franchise and Incentive Model
for Group Replication*

Anthony Murathi, Nelly Otieno,
and Paul Rippey

## The Model

In September 2008, CARE Kenya, with support from the Kenya
Financial Sector Deepening Trust (FSDK) launched a Community Savings and Loans Project pilot designed to test whether
innovative management and incentive systems could lead to large
outreach at low cost per member. CARE's project is simultaneously
testing two innovations. CARE hopes that both innovations will
permit greater outreach at lower cost, through empowering local entrepreneurs and faith-based organizations to do work that
was previously done directly by CARE or other implementers.

The first innovation is to pay all the community-based trainers—the individuals who do the actual work of training groups—
exclusively on a commission basis. These individuals receive
approximately two dollars per group member for all the groups
they form. The trainers receive two-thirds when the group starts
saving, and one-third when the group distributes its assets at the
end of the year in order to ensure that they monitor the groups'
quality over the year. These people are not CARE employees but
independent contractors working purely on commission.

The second innovation is the transfer of some management responsibilities from CARE to two groups of local partners: faith-based organizations and local entrepreneurs (franchisees). The franchisees operate under a memorandum of understanding with CARE, and are recompensed for their work at about three dollars per member.

## On the Ground

As part of the test CARE is also directly managing a small group of trainers; although they are managed by CARE, they also are paid on a commission basis. Currently, CARE is directly managing ten community-based trainers; a group of five churches is responsible for twenty trainers; and four local entrepreneurs—the franchisees—are managing twenty more. Initially, CARE is responsible for the preparation and support of all trainers and provides a great deal of technical assistance and oversight to the faith-based organizations and franchisees. In the future CARE expects to delegate an increasing amount of responsibility to these partners.

Like all the community-based trainers, the ten individuals managed directly by CARE are independent contractors, paid on a commission basis for each group member trained. Many of these trainees are recent graduates of teacher-training colleges who either could not find a teaching job or preferred to work for CARE.

CARE has signed memoranda of understanding with five faith-based organizations—the Catholic Church, the Church of God of East Africa, the Quakers, the Seventh-day Adventists, and the Word of Faith Church. These are the predominant church organization in each district in the area where CARE is working. In each case the churches have set up committees that supervise the trainers and assist with mobilization of new groups. The church committees each manage three or four trainers. They have agreed in writing to publicize their services to everyone, regardless of religious beliefs.

CARE has likewise signed agreements with four franchisees, who in turn supervise groups of trainers. The franchisees—two men and two women—are local business people. One sells agricultural products; another runs a hair salon and sells M-PESA money-transfer services; one owns a bookstore; and one transports goods. The franchisees manage about five community-based trainers each, and most say they could manage twice that number.

## As of Now, and Looking Forward

The initial results, four months after the first groups were formed, are positive. The project is well ahead of its goal of having each trainer form three groups a month—five months into the project, the average was 4.4 groups per trainer. Group quality seems to be very good. Direct field operational costs are now about eleven dollars per member; the goal for the entire project is ten dollars.

CARE will continue to monitor the progress of the experiment carefully. It is bringing in a consultant on franchising to help perfect the agreements with the franchisees and faith-based organizations; in particular, the consultant will help reexamine the remuneration plans and help develop a code of conduct to ensure that the other businesses of the entrepreneurs are kept separate from their savings-group business.

CARE still needs to strengthen its data management and to install safeguards against the possibilities of eventual double counting of members of multiple groups or the creation of fictitious groups. CARE also plans to develop an exit strategy for the regions where it is working. It likewise wants to develop an expansion strategy that will allow it to take advantage of the large networks of faith-based organizations, as well as allowing the most successful franchisees to expand their businesses into other regions.

# Chapter 12

# Market-Led Expansion through Fee-for-Service Agents

JULIE ZOLLMANN AND GUY VANMEENEN

## Introduction

Several organizations are considering commercial models to expand the reach and ensure the sustainability of savings groups beyond short-term, donor-driven projects. Market forces, these organizations believe, play a crucial role in scaling-up savings group services by reducing promoting agencies' operational costs. "Cost per client" may be greatly reduced over time by charging fees to the members for group mobilization, training, and ongoing technical support.

Organizations are now experimenting with training and deploying "fee-for-service agents" who create and support savings groups. These individuals collect fees directly from the groups they support and sometimes receive incentives such as bicycles from the sponsoring organization. While the savings-led microfinance community has largely accepted the underlying logic of fee-for-service agents, important questions remain: What is the best method for training and deploying agents? How can NGOs ensure that fees do not inhibit the participation of the poorest? What support structures are necessary to sustain a system of agents? To what extent should NGOs supervise agents in the long term? CARE, Catholic Relief Services, Plan International, and Pact are forging ahead with fee-for-service models, attempting to uncover answers to these questions.

119

## Program Profiles

### Pact's WORTH program, Nepal

Pact was one of the earliest adopters of the fee-for-service concept. In December 1997 Pact began promoting savings groups in Nepal to enhance its existing women's literacy program. Much like other savings-group programs, members make weekly savings contributions and lend small sums to one another at an agreed-upon interest rate. They also practice literacy skills through reading specially designed written materials that cover financial and business management. Women are expected to cover their own costs for books, a cash box, a calculator, and fees for the services of a literacy volunteer. The decision to charge participation fees was controversial, but demand for the service far exceeded supply.

The program intentionally included a large range of income groups, because staff believed that the comparatively better off would make important financial, intellectual, and social-capital contributions that would enhance the quality of the program. Still, 45 percent of participants were "deeply poor" (spending just $75 per year), and 35 percent were only slightly better off (spending $160).

The WORTH program achieved impressive levels of scale, durability, and impact on women's income. In three years WORTH reached 125,000 women in six thousand savings groups across southern Nepal's Terai region. About fifteen hundred of these groups, with 35,000 members, received additional training in bookkeeping and savings and lending practices, becoming informal "village banks."

The program ended in 2001, and the Maoist insurgency caused serious disruptions in much of the program area. Despite these disruptions, a 2006 study found 64 percent of all village banks still in operation five years after external support ended. Those original groups had formed an additional 425 groups by 2006. There were actually more village-bank members in Nepal in 2007 than there were in 2001, when Pact's WORTH program ended. Interestingly, the overwhelming majority of second-generation groups was not charged for training and did not go on to form third-generation groups.[1]

## CARE Africa

CARE's use of fee-for-service agents began independently in several country offices, including Niger, Tanzania, and Malawi. In Malawi, the concept developed unintentionally. Members from previously trained groups were forming new groups on their own, and members of the new groups made small contributions to these volunteer agents to cover the expense of traveling the necessary long distances to meet different groups. Eventually the concept was integrated into CARE's Save Up program. Funded by the Bill and Melinda Gates Foundation, Save Up seeks to demonstrate effective savings group scale-up strategies in Tanzania, Uganda, and Malawi. Fee-for-service agents are a key part of the expansion strategies used in Tanzania and Malawi.

*Selection:* When CARE begins working in a new area, project staff forms the first round of groups. CARE selects agents from within these staff-trained groups after the groups have been in operation for at least three months. Agents must demonstrate thorough understanding of the methodology, have good facilitation skills, and show leadership ability. Literacy is not a prerequisite, as CARE uses a stamped passbook approach instead of written ledgers. CARE trains the agents in group formation, savings and internal-lending practices, distance-supervision methods, and group graduation requirements. Once agent training is complete, Save Up gives each agent a bicycle.

*Supervision and management:* Initially, field officers intensively supervise trained agents, but the frequency and intensity of supervision decreases over the course of a year. During that year agents are expected to train about eight groups. After that year agents become independent. Agents who have formed groups that function well encourage their members to spread the word about their services. Poorly performing agents soon find that negative word-of-mouth information drives away new business. CARE has found that market forces do, by and large, encourage strong agent performance.

*Value added:* Agents enable the low-cost expansion of savings groups. Agents mobilize and train groups, mentor group-management committees, monitor group performance, assist groups in execution of action audits (end-of-cycle fund liquidation), help resolve group conflicts, and promote new products to groups. If revenue is significant from additional services, agents may choose to slow their formation of new groups; offering additional services to existing clients may be the more profitable option.

*Remuneration*: CARE expects the savings groups to pay the agents. The agent must negotiate an appropriate rate with the groups; CARE suggests agents charge $25 to $50 per group in Tanzania and Malawi. The rate may take the form of a one time, end-of-cycle fee, or a fee for every meeting attended or service provided.

*Monitoring agent effectiveness*: CARE expects to monitor the effectiveness of agents and the agent approach in several dimensions: Purely financial considerations include the sources and amounts of agent income, as well as the fees agents are charging groups compared to the NGO's suggested fee schedule. For service provision CARE looks at the range of services the agent provides and performance comparisons of agent-trained groups versus those trained by paid trainers. CARE also uses survey data derived from both agents and group members.[2]

### Catholic Relief Services, Africa

Catholic Relief Services (CRS) is developing an innovative fee-for-service model through the certification of field agents in Kenya, Uganda, and Tanzania under its grant from the Bill and Melinda Gates Foundation. CRS was interested in expanding savings-group services but had concerns regarding group quality. In nonfee models, members of preexisting groups form new groups, informally and without pay. Would quality decline after each successive generation of groups? The fee-for-service alternative was proposed as a means to wean clients off subsidies, enable savings groups to reach greater scale, and maintain quality through successive generations of group promotion.

CRS defines sustainability at three levels. At the group level, individual groups must be trained and become independent after twelve months and remain active over time. At the agent level, certified agents must be actively supporting new and existing groups on a fee-for-service basis. And at the network level, local networks of agents must ensure a continuous supply of trained agents by assuming responsibility for initial training, apprenticeship, and certification.

*Selection*: CRS identifies agent trainees from program villages, often drawing from existing savings groups. Agents must have good facilitation skills, be able to speak the local dialect, have practical understanding of group dynamics, and—unlike CARE agents—be literate and able to use the agent operations manual. They must also be able to facilitate a hybrid record-keeping system, based on written and oral group records. A local committee screens all prospective candidates and selects promising individuals to participate in a competitive, one-week training course, followed by a final exam. Upon successful completion of every stage, a candidate becomes an agent trainee. Reaching this point is not assured—only 50 to 70 percent of the initial candidates make it.

*Training and certification process (twelve to fifteen months)*: During their first year, trainees work as apprentices, and CRS pays them a fee based on the quality and efficiency of their work. Only trainees who have worked for at least one year under close supervision, who have completed the required training, and who have proved that their savings groups are performing adequately are eligible to take the certification exam. The certification exam, administered by CRS and its local partners, consists of qualitative and quantitative measurements of a trainee's performance.

However, the final exam is not the only form of assessment. Additionally, a client-satisfaction survey assesses the trainee's facilitation and communication skills. A portfolio performance review looks at the quality of the trainee's services, as shown by achieving or exceeding minimum performance standards, such as attendance rates, drop-out rates, return on savings, and so on. Finally, a panel interview uses standard questions to gauge the applicant's technical knowledge and capacity. Trainees meeting certification requirements are designated private service providers, gaining the right to charge new groups for their services. CRS believes this intensive training and certification process ensures that agents provide significant value to groups, while also earning a livelihood. CRS plans to transfer the validated agent training, supervision, and certification process to independent agent networks over a one- to two-year period.

*Value added*: Agents help to form and train groups, teach record-keeping and financial management, connect groups to other service providers, and monitor group performance in order to provide support as groups mature and encounter new challenges. An agent is expected to meet with group members between twenty-two and thirty-five times during the initial one-year cycle. More mature groups are likely to require less frequent, but more specialized, interventions, such as conflict resolution, bylaw review, diversification of savings funds, selection of committee members, share-out, and linkages with other development service providers. Over time, agents may also offer additional services, like agricultural-enterprise development—for an additional fee.

*Remuneration*: Agents earn a living by supporting new and mature groups at a negotiated fee, paid by the groups. Until the trainees are certified, no fees are charged. Once certified, agents charge fees to groups that request assistance. Preliminary research indicates that groups are able to pay an agent $1 to $2 per meeting for training and technical support. At two meetings per day, six days per week, an agent could earn $48 to $96 every month, which is considered a very healthy salary in these rural settings.

### Plan International, Burkina Faso

In Burkina Faso, Plan International encourages women's groups to pay agents to organize and train their groups. Plan practitioners believe that agent services will encourage more rapid replication of groups, because agents have an incentive to expand their reach and train more groups aggressively. Originally, the NGO recruited agents from program communities as volunteers, but more recently savings groups themselves have been footing the bill. Plan suggested a payment schedule of $0.03 per woman per meeting. With an average group size of thirty women, this rate translates into $0.90 per meeting. Each agent supports about five groups, and therefore should earn about $3.40 every week, or every two weeks, depending on meeting frequency. Agents negotiate with each group of clients on the fee schedule. Additionally, like CRS and CARE, Plan provides agents with bicycles to encourage them to expand their reach.

Plan currently trains agents through nine modules on savings-group methodology. The modules focus on organizing group leadership, creating bylaws, and running group meetings for both savings and lending. Plan's field staff supervises, with each staff person responsible for about six agents, who each generally serve about five groups. Agents regularly provide their designated staff supervisor with performance data on groups, a system that enables Plan to track the performance of all groups involved in the project. Staff members also visit groups independently to ensure that agents are meeting the needs of groups, and that groups are running smoothly.[3]

## Prospects and Perils:
## Toward a Learning Agenda

The fee-for-service concept is promising, but it is still untested and unproven. These experiments by CARE, CRS, Pact, and Plan International will reveal additional understanding of five broad issues:

*Balancing quality and control:* By using fee-for-service agents, organizations accept a tradeoff between sustainability and control. How will organizations respond when there are concerns about the quality of agents' work, or low achievement of outreach targets? What if local innovations are out of line with core methodological principles? What will these organizations do with incidences of outright fraud? Independent agents may make extensive changes to savings-group methodologies, which could be either a healthy opportunity for innovation or an erosion of tried-and-tested principles that results in weaker groups.

Additionally, when agents are independent, they have no incentive to report data on group performance to anyone, including the NGOs that trained them. In order to entice agents to report, some organizations are providing agents with transport allowances; CRS will pay $2 to $4 per month. Other NGOs have devised an even more creative strategy. They offer agents the chance to earn additional income through the sale of village savings-and-loan toolkits, usually including three-key lockboxes and passbooks. The agent keeps a share of the revenue, returns a share to the NGO, and in the process of paying the NGO its share, gives the NGO important information.[4]

*Accelerating the pace of scale*: It is not clear that agents will actually accelerate the expansion of savings groups. CARE's early experience in Uganda suggests that agents may lack adequate incentives to achieve aggressive targets set by implementing organizations.[5] CRS handles this problem by concentrating its efforts in geographic areas of up to 100,000 clients in a maximum of two geographic areas per country in order to build a market for savings-group services through the "demonstration effect." The NGO hopes that saturation of the initial geographic areas combined with word-of-mouth marketing will drive more entrepreneurial agents to expand their outreach to other regions of the country.

*De facto cost reductions*: Given considerable up-front investment in agent training, certification, supervision, and support institution building, and the limited geographic reach of each agent, it is not yet clear just how much (if any) cost savings NGOs might realize by using the agent model. The range of services groups receive and the length of time services are available may increase, potentially yielding more "bang" for every donor buck. But these gains are possible only if agents remain motivated, receive news of methodological improvements and advanced services, and actively promote a range of services to groups.

*Maintaining active agents*: Where population density is low and transport costs are high, effective demand for each agent's services may be too low for the agent model to be commercially viable. CRS's experience in Tanzania shows that not all agents in areas with low population density want to use their skills for income generation. Instead, they continue to support groups within the community as volunteers or in exchange for non-cash benefits. Both CRS and CARE are seeking ways to provide agents with more consistent income streams by diversifying the types of services agents may offer.

*Inclusion of the poorest*: Savings-group programs in the past have been concerned about the tendency of their programs to turn away the poorest members of communities due to these individuals' irregular cash flows and social exclusion. However, many of the poorest belong to ROSCAs that pay management fees to the person who organizes the collection and distribution of funds. It is unclear whether the introduction of agent fees to these savings groups will worsen exclusion.

*Consumer protection*: While perhaps the risk is small, it is possible that agents may assume potentially inappropriate or exploitative roles. Literacy rates are very low in many of the areas where these groups thrive. If the agent—who is literate while other group members are not—becomes solely responsible for group accounting, it exposes the group to the risk of error and corruption. CARE insists that groups adapt an accounting method that can be internally managed. CRS is promoting memory-based record-keeping on top of the central ledger, so that group members can check and balance the main accounts. CRS also plans to instruct groups on the appropriate role of agents and will encourage groups to develop rules to protect and limit agent financial participation.

## Conclusion

These NGOs are experimenting with market-led approaches to providing millions of clients with quality services at limited cost. However, it remains to be seen whether these models will be the bridge between donor-driven implementing organizations and a genuine savings-group marketplace. With many questions left unanswered, candid sharing of learning will be critical to shape adaptations and enable the sector to reach aggressive goals for expansion and impact. And still, a broader question remains: Might local commercial replication become a new development model for other development activities, sideline NGOs, and become a sustainable driver for genuine poverty alleviation in rural areas?

## Notes

[1] Valley Research Group and Dr. Linda Mayoux. "Women Ending Poverty: The WORTH Program in Nepal" (Pact, 2008).

[2] Grace Majara, email with the authors, January 2009; Mark Staehle, email with the authors, July 2009.

[3] John Schiller, email with Helen Ho, former intern, Plan Burkina Faso, December 2008.

[4] Majara.

[5] Ibid.

Chapter 13

# The Green Box

*The Savings Systems of Smallholder Farmers in Southern Haiti*

KIM WILSON AND GAYE BURPEE

## Introduction

As most of the Western Hemisphere climbs toward further stability and prosperity, Haiti continues to slip into instability and poverty. Over three-fourths of the nation's 8.3 million people live on less than $2 a day. More than half live on less than $1 a day.[1]

Watershed areas in the southern peninsula take a particular beating. Sixty-eight percent of households live below the poverty line, enduring regular and devastating hurricanes and recurring periods of drought. Hard-hitting storms, degraded soils, and diminished forests leave residents and their small plots of land—most under 0.65 hectares, or about 1.6 acres—vulnerable to rain and wind, and ensuing floods and mudslides. Working the fields or trawling the over-fished shores has become difficult, and a single hurricane can erase any gains made by households living among the steep, tree-bare hills that line the coast.

Despite these hardships, 66 percent of the work force still farms for a living. Haitian households raise livestock; grow fruit trees; cultivate wheat and corn and vegetable crops like cabbage, eggplant, beets, and sweet potatoes. They also sell snacks, fruit, fish, clothes, and candy, or run small shops and eateries. It was in the spirit of understanding smallholder farmers in Haiti's south that the authors came across savings groups.

Initial market research conducted by Catholic Relief Services in September 2007 showed that poor financial services—in terms of availability and quality—were a barrier to increasing the value of farm outputs and rural enterprise. To better understand difficulties and opportunities, CRS, along with Tufts University, returned that November to explore available credit and savings options. The researchers interviewed 134 men and women, including those in farmers' clubs, parent-teacher associations, mothers' health clubs, savings clubs, NGOs, churches, and microfinance institutions.

## Microfinance in the Southern Peninsula

The microfinance sector has grown in Haiti, but less so in rural areas. In the coastal areas to the west of the southern town of Les Cayes, a network of credit unions is helping to improve the financial landscape, but many households still pawn their valuables to fund weddings, school fees, and burials. Microfinance institutions seemed most unwelcome. Residents complained bitterly about their high interest rates, rigid loan terms, and ruthless collection practices.

Households reported using variations of ROSCAs as a source of funds. While those in the marketplace, called *sabatayes*, accept daily deposits and disbursals, others, known as *sol,* accept monthly deposits and are a more common system among farm families.

For example, in the remote hamlet of Morsseau, a *sol* of sixteen women cultivate land and buy and sell rice, plantains, clothes, and utensils. Each Saturday, members meet to contribute seventy-five gourds (around $2.10) for a total pool of $33. After getting their payouts or lump sums, some members use the money to buy clothes or snacks to trade, and others purchase small household items such as pots and pans for household use. Recently, the *sol* funded the cost of a burial for a fellow villager.

While these do-it-yourself solutions help families turn small flows of cash into more useful sums of cash, they lack flexibility. Those interviewed expressed a need for better services. "It is not enough," said one *sol* member. This particular *sol* already had plans to transform into a *mutuelle*.

## A Rainbow of Boxes

One financial concept—emergent and rapidly expanding—is the *mutuelle*, a form of ASCA that offers three financial services: savings, credit, and insurance. *Mutuelles* vary from nine to sixty members. Members of *mutuelles* gather to make regular savings deposits into a group fund and then disburse small loans to members at the same meeting. Unlike the *sol*, where each member takes a turn at receiving the entire fund, multiple members of a *mutuelle* receive small loans and repay them over time. Regular savings deposits and loan interest help the fund grow. Once a year, usually, all loans outstanding are repaid, the cash is counted, and the funds are distributed back to members according to their savings and interest earned. The fund starts afresh, sometimes immediately, with each member depositing much of the payout from the last round as her initial savings in the new round.

*Mutuelles* were the brainchild of Bernard Taillefer. After forming and studying similar groups in Africa for years, Taillefer came to Haiti under the auspices of COD-EMH, an NGO of the Methodist Church, and SIDI, a French donor. He trained members of churches and NGOs in a series of intensive, and evidently quite memorable, workshops.

In Port-Au-Prince, organizations that promoted *mutuelles*, and trained under Taillefer, told us that they taught members to keep their accounts in three separate boxes, one painted green, another red, and a third blue.

The green box was the financial heart and soul of the *mutuelle*, made up of savings—hard-won from the hands of customers and employers, from overseas relatives sending money home, and even from spouses and children. The green box was also the symbol of financial discipline: loans cautiously distributed and diligently repaid. Members would gather monthly to make deposits into the green box, a sum pegged to the savings capacity of the *mutuelle*'s poorest member. Monthly contributions would range from about $0.84 to $1.45 per member. The green-box committee (essentially a loan-approval committee) would disburse credit to members, basing its decisions on member need and capacity to repay.

The red box would supply emergency cash: money to buy medicine for a sick child, a sudden trip to the doctor, or a funeral. Red box disbursals were usually made as grants; members who received the emergency amounts did not need to repay them. Red boxes were funded in a variety of ways, as each *mutuelle* saw fit. Some *mutuelles* would set aside a portion of the interest earned from the internal savings and lending in their green boxes for the red box, or would allocate 10 percent of their regular green-box contributions to pump a steady flow of cash into the red box. Still other groups periodically passed the hat in a separate red-box collection.

The blue box was for loans that might come from banks, NGOs, credit unions, or microfinance institutions to supplement *mutuelle* savings. For example, if *mutuelle* members were able to save $100, their blue box might warrant another $200 from a local bank. The *mutuelle* would then have $300 to lend to its members.

But our interviews in the south of Haiti, five or six hours by road from Port-Au-Prince, showed a variation on the colorful boxes. *Mutuelles* did indeed keep their funds separate, and members logged details in green, red, and blue notebooks. But the colorful boxes were nowhere in sight. A *mutuelle* treasurer said: "The brightly painted boxes attract too much attention. We prefer to carry our money to meetings hidden in our clothes or tucked under our hats. In the meetings we pass around different hats or bowls to signify the green and red boxes."

"What about the blue box?" we asked. "The one that is to take additional credit from banks or credit unions to supplement your green-box funds." Responded one member: "Blue is the color of wishing. We wish, of course, to have the blue box filled, but that has not happened. So for now, we focus on growing the green box."

## The Green Box and Its Loans

Loan terms vary. Members use one-month loans for small trading and household consumption. Six-month loans help purchase seeds and fertilizer, tools, and fishing equipment, or pay school tuitions and buy books and uniforms. Interest rates set by the groups range between 2 and 5 percent a month, depending on the group's goal for fund accumulation and its members' savings capacity.

*Mutuelles* have found clever ways to boost regular savings and loans by establishing special funds for special purchases. For example, all fifteen members of one group agreed that each member should own a cow. Through a special-purpose fund that amasses an additional $200–$270 per cycle, ten members have purchased cows and five have locked in prices and purchase dates with livestock suppliers.

Some green boxes have grown beyond $2,900 during an eight-year period. Loans support small trading activities, agriculture, horticulture, home improvement and, increasingly, the use of cell phones. Said one member: "My cell phone is another pair of legs and another pair of arms." Members use their phones to check on children and make arrangements with friends. Those who trade for a living use them to compare costs from suppliers. The lucky few who have relatives in the United States sending them money use their phones to get the news that their remittance is safe and waiting for pickup at a local Western Union agent or a small shop.

Members insisted that one of the most common uses of loans was to pay school fees. Tuition fees in the south vary depending on the school, whether it is public or private. To give the reader an idea, sixth-grade tuitions run about $28 per semester, and some secondary and high school fees reach $56 per semester. However, the problem of tuition is not always its high price. Many members said that though they were poor, they could generally afford the fees, including the costs of uniforms and books that accompanied tuition.

The issue for these members was timing. Farming households receive an influx of cash after the late-autumn grain harvests or after Christmas festivals. But school starts in September. "Sometimes we keep our children out of school until January, until we have the cash," one interviewee explained. "We hope they catch up." But four months of missed school is often four months too many. Children repeat grades or drop out altogether. In September many members use green-box loans to bridge the gap between tuition due dates and household cash flows, which spike several months later. Because not all members have children in school, the green box has ample coffers to fund tuition loan requests, particularly when the group has been accumulating deposits for several years.

## Who Is Making This Happen?

Perhaps among Bernard Taillefer's most dedicated protegees are several women working for the social development organization Caritas-DCCH (Development Comunitaire Chretien Haitien), based in Les Cayes. These part-time promoters see *mutuelles* as a way to support their work with women's groups in health, education, human rights, and advocacy against sexual violence. *Mutuelles*, as they understand them, solve a host of problems.

First, *mutuelles* help keep women safe. Rigid loan terms from local microfinance institutions were pulling women off their farms in search of money for repayments. One *mutuelle* promoter said that the frequent repayments, high interest rates—often more than 4 percent a month—and short loan cycles were a deadly brew for poor farm households. She went on to say, "Women cannot repay the fixed payments from their agricultural cash flow, so they leave the fields and enter petty trading where cash streams in daily, helping to make frequent loan repayments." This shift from the farm to towns, she explains, leaves women vulnerable to violence and petty street crime. Since *mutuelles* structure their own loans, they can build in flexibility for agricultural uses, such as repayment terms that match cash from the harvest. "When women are able to borrow for agriculture, they are less likely to abandon their farms."

Second, *mutuelles* help women turn income into assets. Depositing into the green box allows women to store small inflows of cash—cash that otherwise might trickle out of the household in many small, nearly invisible expenses, such as the frequent purchase of tickets at the local lottery. For example, several *mutuelles* interviewed had records that showed each member contributed $2.86 per month. This may seem like a small amount, but after just a year they had $571 in savings and an additional $137 in interest and fees. Members in this *mutuelle* used their loans to process fruit into candy, to grow bananas, and to purchase and sell food, clothes, and household goods. They also bought seed and fertilizer to improve yields of sorghum and plant vegetables.

Third, *mutuelles* build a sense of self-reliance and a sense of cooperation. One NGO worker described groups that told her that "the *mutuelle* is our second husband." In Les Cayes a group member similarly remarked, laughing, "We are married to our groups, and they make better husbands than the men we married."

Fourth, *mutuelles* provide the financial underpinnings of further social action and development. As group funds build, members begin expanding economic activities, leading to more funds for the group. For example, the parent-teacher association of St. Dominic's School in Coteaux formed a *mutuelle* into which PTA members make regular deposits and take out loans of $112 to $140. Members use the loans jointly to trade coconut, corn, sorghum and sweet potato, all with funds from the green box. After damage from a hurricane, this *mutuelle* used a combination of red- and green-box funds and their own labor to make repairs to the local school. Members have plans to help other PTAs in towns nearby to form new *mutuelles*.

## Go Forth and Multiply

Together, the Caritas-DCCH staff has formed 702 *mutuelles* with a total of 10,500 members. Three part-time staff members oversee these groups. While it was difficult to disaggregate *mutuelle* formation costs from other development work, Caritas-DCCH estimated that forming and strengthening *mutuelles* came to less than $0.50 per member per year, a number that compares favorably to microfinance institution costs per borrower, reported by the MixMarket in December 2007 at between $72 and $372.

How could the three women of Caritas-DCCH, working part time to form *mutuelles*, reach so many women (and men) in locales off the road and off cellular and power grids? Caritas-DCCH staff decided early on that if they were to form each and every *mutuelle*, the concept could not expand, or at least not quickly. They lacked the resources to add more staff. If *mutuelles* were going to multiply, staff would need to be strategic.

Their first strategy was to build on existing clubs and organizations. NGO staff began by converting mothers' clubs for health purposes into *mutuelles*. Mothers' clubs either had no savings plan in place or conducted savings on the *sol* system. Slowly *sols* and clubs transformed into *mutuelles* that took in deposits and gave out loans. These "converts" were to become the backbone of expansion.

Their second strategy was to encourage *mutuelles* to multiply. Residents who were not in a *mutuelle* began to notice those who were in one. Non-members saw how active *mutuelle* members had become, how they debated loan rules for hours, sometimes well into the night, how they would lend a hand in emergencies, and how their savings grew steadily. Motivated, interested community members asked Caritas for help in setting up their own *mutuelles*. Caritas staff, if they could spare the time, helped start a new *mutuelle*. If not, they sent interested families to a neighboring *mutuelle* for advice. Over the years existing *mutuelles* passed on their lessons to new ones. *Mutuelles* now carpet some areas, with a member of every family a member of at least one *mutuelle*.

Interestingly, no part of their strategy included the development of a manual. The organizers were too busy organizing to take time to develop a manual that would forever turn what had been a fluid form of assistance into a fixed manifesto. Finally, after seven years, the team produced a three-page document of lessons and tips.

## Guarding the Green Box

"Thieves can take the money and run. So can group members," said one promoter. "But, that hasn't happened to us." If outright thievery is not a prevalent problem, what is? The biggest threat to a *mutuelle*'s money is financial illiteracy. If *mutuelle* members do not understand the value of their savings or their liabilities, they are subject to exploitation or inaccurate accounting.

To reduce the potential for mistakes, at each meeting the treasurer repeats aloud the amount that each member is depositing, paying back, or receiving; group members must verify by verbal agreement—an oral "yes."

For eight years groups have reported no trouble with members stealing funds. The main concern of members was fire or theft by outsiders. "Always collect payments and make disbursals in the same meeting," was an oft-repeated mantra. Some *mutuelle* members would gather to take in payments in the evening and then rush home before dark to prepare the evening meal. They would regroup the next day to make loan disbursals, leaving the treasurer to guard the green box (a real or figurative box) overnight. One evening a fire broke out in a treasurer's home, which happily did not damage the cash. But the event signaled a need for immediate disbursement upon collection.

"The real protection," says Pere Tilus, director of Caritas, Haiti, "is the concept itself. In *mutuelles*, everyone knows each other. No one can pass the buck, or blame a bank manager or a credit-union manager. If anything goes wrong, each member knows he or she has responsibility."

## Clustering for Social Action

With the help of their organizing NGO, in this case Caritas-DCCH, some *mutuelles* cluster into associations. Associations do not intermediate funds but exist to help member *mutuelles* resolve problems or tackle social issues. In one association members came together to petition the judiciary and demand that all children receive legal birth certificates. Without a birth certificate, individuals cannot access other rights (voting) or services (medical care). Another association helped defend the rights of a child. A local policeman, purportedly, had raped her, and it seemed as if there was no recourse. The *mutuelle* relentlessly pestered local officials and politicians, and even served as the child's lawyer. The police officer is now in prison.

Caritas-DCCH staff claim associations help use staff time effectively. If three *mutuelles* meet at the same time, staff can reach roughly three times the people with similar messages in health or empowerment. Associations can also form new *mutuelles*, further reducing staff time and cost of expanding *mutuelles*. The team's hope is to reach the services of *mutuelles* into every hill and hollow along Haiti's southern coast.

## Why the Success?

We were struck by the simplicity and the performance of the Caritas-DCCH effort in forming *mutuelles*. The very fact that *mutuelle* promotion was never funded as a project may partially explain its success. Forming *mutuelles* was just something useful that helped the organization achieve a higher set of goals, namely empowerment, financial well-being, and civic action.

Accounting for a high staff-to-member ratio was the unflagging commitment of staff. But the women organizers were a tough lot, not inclined to pat themselves on the back. When asked how they would rate their *mutuelles*, one said: "B's and C's. No A's. When we see an A, we'll let you know."

Perhaps, too, good performance was a result of the few motivational trainings run by Bernard Taillefer, low on manuals and written guides and high on inspiration and the most essential "how-tos." These factors blended to create an approach that is flexible, useful, colorful—at least in the mind's eye—and low cost. Indeed, they have earned an A.

## Afterword

In January 2012 Haiti was struck by a powerful, devastating earthquake. In the months that followed one of the authors kept in close touch with a *mutuelle*, Brave Warriors (Vayan Konbatant), in Port-Au-Prince. Members had lost family and shelter yet continued to meet every Thursday evening to collect loan repayments and to make new loans. Just one week after the earthquake, one member borrowed from the green box to fund a new business selling airtime for mobile phones. She reports that her business is doing well. She adds that Brave Warriors is starting a new *mutuelle* for children.

## Note

1. The devastating earthquake that hit Haiti on January 12, 2010, has of course made life even harder for its people.

Chapter 14

# Adapting the *Bachat* Committee

*Helping Pakistan's Urban and Rural Poor Save Better*

### WAJIHA AHMED

While credit and microloans to the rural and urban poor can have both positive and negative effects, it is hard to find any downside to providing savings services. Savings help the poor increase their financial resilience to shocks and reduce their dependency on loans and patronage. Realizing the potential of savings, many poor people in the developing world have themselves formed ROSCAs. In Pakistan, these associations are referred to as *bachat* committees, or saving committees. *Bachat* committees collect money over a specified period of time and offer the whole pot to one member on a rotating basis.

Leveraging this local practice, the First MicroFinance Bank Ltd. of Pakistan (the "Bank") has created an innovative and simple strategy to promote a community savings product called the Contractual Savings Product. To participate in this program, clients form groups of three to thirty-five people and save monthly for a predetermined period. Currently, the Bank offers savings in various increments ranging from $0.10 to $12 for periods ranging from one month up to four years; interest income as well as a life-insurance policy are included.

The savings-deposit process is simple. A group leader deposits the collective savings with the Bank. The Bank credits each group member's original contribution to individual checking accounts and then automatically transfers the balances to individual savings accounts. Savings are voluntary, but if a client chooses to withdraw from his or her account, the Bank terminates the savings contract, transferring the balance back into the checking account, from which the client is able to withdraw the funds. The Bank also cancels all incurred interest and the insurance policy. Clients can subsequently reapply for a new account, provided they form a new group.

The product has gained popularity and expanded rapidly. When bank branches introduced the Contractual Savings Product in 2008, almost a thousand new clients signed on every month. As of January 2009, sixty-eight of the Bank's eighty-nine nationwide branches offered the product in Pakistan's Northern Areas as well as in Chitral, Punjab, and Sindh. The service is reaching 1,626 active committees and 7,203 individual savers, with a total balance of $96,513. In a country where the working poor often make no more than $30 a month, individual savings averaging $46 provide an important safety net.[1]

While similar to the *bachat* committee, the Contractual Savings Product is superior in a few key areas. Most important, group members gain a secure place to store their money. All too often the working poor store what little cash they have in boxes or secret places around the house. It is hard to save when the cash is so available. It can stream out of the home in the form of many small expenses. As Bilquees Bibi, a client in Lahore, explains, "I want to develop the saving habit in myself, and it is not possible to save money at home."

Clients earn a market return on their savings accounts, currently around 7 percent. Additionally, in the case of a client's death, the bank links the product with an insurance policy. For a small monthly premium, as low as $0.25, clients can insure the uncollected contracted amount of savings over the specified period. In case of a natural death the client's beneficiaries receive the full amount of savings specified in the contract, and in the case of an accidental death the family receives a lump sum of $500. Bushra Bibi from Lahore, who aims to save $30, expressed her appreciation for the insurance product: "I like the insurance feature the most," she said. "It feels good to have a bank account knowing I am saving money for unseen emergencies. If something happens to me, my beneficiaries have some funds to help pay for services or whatever they might need."

Savers are not required to attend regular meetings, which can be burdensome and taxing for the time-pressed working poor. The Bank has also broken free from the conventional microfinance paradigm of working exclusively with women—almost half of its contractual savers are men.

While 68 percent of savings clients run their own businesses, many, like Bibi Maqnoon from Gilgit, set aside money for several purposes: "I am saving for my daughter's wedding," she declared, "and after that I'll save to improve my house."

Like traditional microfinance borrowers, 48 percent of clients are saving to grow their businesses, but 24 percent are collecting money for education expenses and 6 percent are saving in preparation for unforeseen health problems. Students saving for school expenses make up 4 percent of the loan portfolio. Many mothers are saving for their children's education.

Recently, Pakistan's economic crisis and growing inflation problem have taken a toll on the new savings product. The poor are saving less, slowing the product's growth. Still, it is hoped that their savings can help mitigate the effects of the economic recession.

## Note

[1] Ayesha Baig, email with the author, March 2009.

Qiamuddin Amiry

Savings group member in Bamyan Province, Afghanistan,
contributes monthly savings to the
designated group accountants.

# PART 4

---

# SINKING, SWIMMING, AND STAYING AFLOAT

Savings group promotion is big business. It costs a lot of money and is increasingly touted as a cost-effective new approach to poverty reduction, or more modestly but perhaps more accurately, to financial inclusion. The agencies that promote savings groups, and the donors that pay them to do it, need to know if their money is being well spent, if there are cheaper ways of achieving the same or better results, and if the groups are doing their members any good.

The articles in this section summarize studies of the phenomenon, and they even provide a glimpse of the long-term results of three sets of savings groups. They include two rather unusual examples of groups in remote mountainous areas in Nepal and Northern Pakistan, where the promotion agency has more or less withdrawn so that the groups have been compelled to "sink or swim" on their own.

First, Marcia Odell's chapter describes the results of a study of groups in Nepal. These groups had been promoted in Nepal by Pact International, but the program was interrupted for five years by a guerrilla war that led to the overthrow of the monarchy and the halt to funds. The condition of their groups after this gap suggests that premature termination of donor projects may be a good thing, at least in savings-group promotion.

143

In Chapter 16 Wajiha Ahmed and Joanna Ledgerwood describe the results of the Aga Khan Rural Support Programme's promotion of groups in Northern Pakistan. The AKRSP was one of the earliest large agencies to promote savings-led microfinance, and part of its program was converted into a bank specializing in microfinance in 2001. This transition meant that much of the close support for the groups was withdrawn. The consequences were both surprising (groups grew in size) and not surprising (many groups continued to function well).

Last, In Chapter 17, Eloisa Devietti and Janina Matuszeski describe a qualitative study of ten groups promoted by Oxfam America in its Savings for Change program in El Salvador. The study identified the problem of dependency on handouts in over-aided communities and the problem of studying the impact of groups without a good baseline to precede the promotion of groups. The authors seem to think that group members are not borrowing enough from their savings funds, that lending levels are low. But the editors question whether encouraging members to borrow is a good idea, or if it is a reflection of "our" notion of what a successful group is.

Many important impact issues have not been touched. None of our authors asks whether group members might have started a similar savings group, or perhaps a ROSCA, on their own, without any outside promotion. None has learned whether members are already part of a ROSCA or ASCA and simply diverted savings to the newly promoted group. None has tackled the issue of the opportunity cost of the service—might it have been better to give the money in cash to the members rather than spend it on training them in group formation and management? Or might the money have been better spent on medical care or children's education?

But, generally, savings-group promotion seems to be a good deal, certainly when judged by the start-up costs of microfinance institutions or other foreign donor programs. If it is done well, it is also efficient by the more demanding standards of good local programs.

Chapter 15

# Women's Empowerment through Literacy, Banking, and Business

*The WORTH Program in Nepal—*
*Post-Program Research Findings*

MARCIA L. ODELL

## Introduction

WORTH is a women's empowerment program that combines business, banking, and literacy—a savings-led program in which women become social activists, social entrepreneurs, and effective leaders in their communities. Initially known as the Women's Empowerment Program, Pact conducted WORTH in Nepal for two and a half years between 1999 and 2001, reaching 125,000 women in six thousand groups across southern Nepal. Approximately fifteen hundred of these groups received training to become informal-sector "Village Banks" (savings groups that function as ASCAs). As the Maoist insurgency gained momentum in 2001 and the priorities of the donor, USAID, changed, the program ended. This left the WORTH groups, including Village Banks, entirely on their own.

In 2006, as the Maoist insurgency began to subside, Pact asked women's empowerment specialist Linda Mayoux, in collaboration with the Valley Research Group in Kathmandu, to find out what happened to the Village Banks. The study would determine if any of the 1,500 Village Banks still existed, despite the civil war and the collapse of national government, and, if so, how they were faring as community banks and as vehicles of change. The study was intended to explore how WORTH affected women's ability to create wealth, and whether or not the groups had taken on broader roles in the community.

In early 2007 seven Nepali research teams fanned out across the 500-mile-wide Terai region in four-wheel-drive vehicles, rickshaws, "tempos," and on foot. Their search uncovered 288 operating Village Banks—plus another 45 banks that WORTH women, on their own, had helped to start. The teams conducted in-depth interviews with Village Bank members and with members of each group's management committee. The teams also interviewed women who had left their Village Banks; members of groups that had dissolved; and poor, non-participating women in Village Bank communities.

## WORTH's Approach and Philosophy

Offering women the chance to become literate is at the heart of WORTH's commitment to women's empowerment. When women can read and write, it is easier for them to access information they can use to improve their lives and ultimately to appreciate how capable they are. Accordingly, WORTH's implementation was built around a series of "easy readers" that women could use together in their groups. These books introduced the sounds and letters of the local language and provided reading practice with content that targeted the development of strong groups, the operation of Village Banks, and the development and management of individual small businesses. Because women read these books together in their groups, they learned together about topics relevant to their success. They could then make informed decisions about their Village Banks, as well as their other businesses.

Another distinguishing element of WORTH's approach was an innovative group process methodology, Appreciative Planning and Action. This methodology encouraged women to focus on their successes rather than their problems and to share stories as a foundation for learning. The Appreciative Planning and Action process enabled women—perhaps for the first time—to listen to the success stories of their peers and to gain both a sense of their own potential and the confidence to try new things. Women shared their stories, achievements, aspirations, and plans for the future in their meetings, as well as through regularly organized family days that involved their families and other community members.

Groups also participated in monthly mobile workshops in which two members from each of ten groups came together to share stories, to ask questions of one another, and to receive additional training. These workshops were enormously popular with the women and helped create informal support networks of Village Banks throughout the program area.

Interspersed among the various WORTH activities in Nepal was a six-month-long Rights, Responsibilities, and Advocacy program delivered by The Asia Foundation. This module, which complemented WORTH's empowerment agenda and the Appreciative Planning and Action process, made use of trained facilitators, focused on a rights-based framework for learning, and promoted the notion that women have both the opportunity and responsibility to be active members of civil society. As an outcome of the training many groups developed action plans to achieve their goals and to bring about change in their communities.

## Key Research Findings

The study showed extremely promising results in terms of the sustainability of the Village Banks, even without WORTH support. Groups also had been replicating themselves, literacy rates of members had increased, and members had continued to involve themselves in wider development-and-advocacy efforts.

As a backdrop, it should be noted that USAID had asked WORTH to target rural women in the Terai, not poor women specifically, and hence not all participants were on the lowest rung of the economic ladder. An evaluation of the program in

2001 concluded, however, that WORTH was particularly attractive to poor women, with 45 percent of participants judged to be poor, subsisting on less than $75 per year, and another 35 percent considered "emerging poor," earning, at most, $160 a year. Only 20 percent were judged to be "better off."[1]

While all the initial participants may not have been among the poorest, both the 2001 evaluation and 2007 research indicated that WORTH members spontaneously brought women poorer than themselves into their groups. The 2007 study revealed that nearly 10 percent of new members coming into a group were generally poorer than the average group member, while slightly less than 1 percent was better off.

## Five Major Findings

### Sustainability

The WORTH Village Banks in Nepal survived years of turbulence, violence, and instability. Management committees in over three-quarters of the operating Village Banks attributed their success to group dynamics—mutual trust among the members, reliance on a consensus-based decision-making process, and a sense of cooperation among members. Three-fifths credited continued operation to their ability to save, which enabled the women to take out loans.

A substantial number of groups reported that they had made considerable progress since WORTH support ended in 2001. For example, half the groups reported that learning how to do business had increased, while 55 percent indicated that literacy had increased. Two-thirds reported increased incomes from businesses, while almost 90 percent reported that both saving and lending had increased since formal programming ended.

Not only had these Village Banks survived, but group membership had grown, from an average of 23.1 members in 2001 to 26.6 in 2007. Furthermore, nearly three-quarters of the groups reported that other community women were seeking membership—an average of 3.9 women for each group. Village Banks also reported that three-quarters of their members had belonged to their groups for at least five years.

Nonetheless, a small proportion of women had dropped out of Village Banks. Management committee members commented on reasons for these women's departure. They reported that the most prominent reasons were marriage (which requires that women move to the village of their husband), or the desire to pursue higher education. Another commonly cited reason was the inability to save at the rate set by the group. Finally, a small percentage left because of objections from their husbands or other family members.

At the same time, nearly 90 percent of the former members who were interviewed said they had benefited from being in the group. Of these, 90 percent reported that the membership experience had helped them to save, and three-fifths said that the group had provided advice and support when they needed help personally. Over half reported that the group had offered new friendships. When asked if they might rejoin the group in the future, 46 percent of the respondents answered "yes" or "probably."

### Replication

Women were enthusiastic about WORTH and generous in devoting their scarce time and resources to the creation of new Village Banks. While the majority of the new groups were formed by WORTH women reaching out on their own to others, a significant number of new groups resulted from women approaching existing groups for help. Not one group said that it would not be interested in supporting the further spread of WORTH.

Even though women in WORTH formed many new groups, few replicated groups had used any WORTH books in the process of becoming Village Banks. In the cases where only some books were available to a new group, management committee members did not always provide adequately for their wide circulation. The availability and cost of new books may have been major constraints on women wanting to create new Village Banks.

Virtually none of the replicated groups paid anything in cash or in kind for the services provided by the original WORTH group. In the judgment of most of the management committees interviewed, the most important advice given to new groups was about saving. They also reported that business skills, good record-keeping, and literacy were important. Seventy-three percent said learning to start or grow businesses was very important; 83 percent said learning to keep good records was very important; and 94 percent reported that learning to read and write was very important.

### Wealth creation

With nearly 70 percent of the Village Banks holding assets in excess of $1,470 in 2007—compared to 20 percent of the groups in 2001—WORTH women had clearly made significant strides in lifting themselves out of poverty. Indeed, nine out of ten groups reported that their economic situation had improved because of WORTH; half of these said it had "greatly improved" because of the program. Another nine out of ten reported that, as a result of WORTH activities, women were better able to provide for the needs of their families. Management committee members estimated that WORTH had helped virtually all group members improve their family well-being, citing indicators such as increased family income, improved access to health care, and enhanced ability to provide adequate food for their families.

Women valued WORTH's focus on literacy and their increasing capacity to educate their children. WORTH is very unusual among both credit- and savings-led microfinance programs in that it places special emphasis on literacy. Women reported that, thanks to this emphasis, they sent more of their children—including their daughters—to school, helped other women learn to read and write, and sometimes took increased responsibility for family and community finances. Half of the respondents specifically named literacy when asked what had changed in their lives as a result of WORTH.

Similarly, learning to read and write ranked highest among all the elements that women named as important aspects of group participation; nearly one-quarter of the women reported that acquiring these skills was the best outcome of the program. Forty-three percent of Bank members reported having been unable to read or write their own names before WORTH; this had shrunk to 8 percent by 2007.

*Community action*
*and social campaigns*

By 2007 many Village Bank members had become leaders in their communities. More than 95 percent of the management committees said that their groups had undertaken social action of some kind. Half reported organizing local social and human-rights campaigns. Responses from interviews with the commit-tees of the 288 Village Banks revealed that groups were providing local emergency assistance, working to reduce discrimination, directing group funds toward charitable purposes, and drawing on group support to cope with the war.

In addition, a significant proportion of the groups reported that since joining WORTH, some of their members had become leaders of other groups. About one-fourth had conducted lit-eracy classes or taught adult-education classes, advocated for women's rights, settled conflicts, or advocated on behalf of women victims of abuse. A similar proportion of groups reported that members had helped teach friends and neighbors to start a busi-ness, or had conducted house-to-house campaigns to promote compulsory girls' education.

Village Bankers played an important role in community after community in dealing with domestic disputes and violence. Forty-three percent of groups reported that their members suffered less domestic violence because of membership in a WORTH group. Women in nearly 10 percent of the groups reported that WORTH had helped "change their life" because of its impact on domestic violence.

Anecdotal evidence supported these findings. When asked what they hoped to gain if they participated in a WORTH pro-gram, Cambodian women visiting a Nepali Village Bank reported that domestic violence was a huge problem in their country. The Cambodians said that perhaps if women could change their role in their family and community by increasing their income or becoming literate, they could successfully tackle this crucial chal-lenge. The response from the Nepali WORTH women was im-mediate: "Domestic abuse is a serious problem in Nepal, too, and it used to be a problem in our village, but now, because of [our group], we don't have that problem here anymore."

## Additional Significant Findings

### Successful management practices continued after Pact's departure

Pact had expected that, after six years, significant changes—even deterioration—would have occurred in the management and accounting systems as WORTH groups struggled to survive Nepal's economic and political ordeals. Even if groups survived, it was assumed likely that their operations and performance would not meet original program standards.

In fact, the operations of Village Banks had remained stable, and groups had retained their management and accounting practices. The groups had not rotated their members through management positions as Pact had recommended, but given the responses of women from dissolved groups or who had left a group, this decision did not appear to have diminished the success of the Village Banks. Furthermore, with no ready source of WORTH accounting forms, Village Banks had improvised their own record-keeping measures; these simplified the original system but did not lead to corruption or fraud.

### Successful loan repayments, even on nonbusiness loans

About 95 percent of Village Banks reported that they had experienced no bad debts since WORTH ended in 2001. Only sixteen management committees (6 percent) reported that they had written off any loans since 2001. This low number is particularly noteworthy given that not all loans were used for demonstrably productive purposes. A fifth of the Village Bank management committees reported that there were "a couple" of members behind in repaying their loans. The average amount that those banks did not expect to be repaid from loans given in the last twelve months was $27 dollars, just over 1 percent of the amount lent out by all the Village Banks during the year.

The WORTH training materials encouraged Village Banks to lend only for business investment, to give borrowers the best chance of being able to pay back their loans on time. Although nearly 90 percent of women reported starting or expanding economic activities as members of their Village Bank, it was not unusual for women to borrow for a variety of other purposes and needs. Notably, women borrowed for education expenses, to meet health needs, or simply to purchase food, particularly early in the program.

### Networking among WORTH groups

Even without formal WORTH programming, Village Banks continued to develop and maintain relationships with each other, cementing informal networks formed during project implementation. Intergroup activities took many forms: More than half of the Village Banks shared ideas and experiences with one another; one-third provided technical support to one another; and one-quarter undertook social or advocacy campaigns with other groups.

### Self-confidence

Women's self-confidence clearly increased as a result of the WORTH program. Nearly all management committee members reported that they were more involved as leaders in their families and communities than they had been previously. Additionally, because of WORTH, 48 percent reported they were better able to discuss a variety of issues and had more interactions with others; they had increased their mobility and enjoyed greater self-confidence and ability to make decisions.

## Conclusion

Taken together, these research findings show WORTH to be remarkably robust and resilient in the hands of women who, for almost a decade and in the face of daunting obstacles, demonstrated their ability and commitment to bring change to their communities. It is clear that with literacy, with the development of Village Banks and other businesses, and with the support of their groups, women can change how they see themselves and how others see them. As women gain self-confidence, provide more fully for their families, challenge cultural norms in their villages, and work to bring other women the benefits of WORTH, the foundation is in place for fundamental change that might be viewed as a quiet revolution.

## Note

¹ Jeffrey Ashe and Lisa Parrott, *Impact Evaluation: Pact's Women's Empowerment Program in Nepal—A Savings and Literacy Led Alternative to Financial Institution Building* (Waltham, MA: Institute for Sustainable Development, Heller School, Brandeis University, 2001).

Chapter 16

# Savings Groups and Village Development in Pakistan's Karakoram Mountain Range

WAJIHA AHMED AND JOANNA LEDGERWOOD

## The Aga Khan Rural Support Program

In the early 1980s the AKRSP encouraged farmers in Pakistan's rugged and poverty-stricken Northern Areas to form groups and begin saving money. Today, well over four thousand groups have accumulated an impressive $8 million in savings, and The Aga Khan Foundation has gone on successfully to replicate its model in other Asian countries.[1]

This chapter draws on a recent assessment of these groups, which included qualitative interviews with seven Village Organizations (member-based groups consisting of the majority of families in the village), thirteen Women's Organizations (groups consisting of only women), project staff members, individual group members, and other relevant stakeholders. Our study concluded that access to financial services at the community level helped Northern Area farmers to manage their household finances and investments through an emphasis on long-term savings, particularly for the promotion of children's higher education. Gradually, the groups also contributed to mitigating sociocultural norms that discriminate against women. Achievements notwithstanding, many groups also exhibited systemic problems related to the management of financial services, such as corruption, continued low levels of financial awareness, and "elite capture," where more powerful members of a community seize control of a group.

Our study recorded a few additional insights. We concluded that when AKRSP ended audits and other forms of support to the Village Organizations in 2001, many groups gradually stopped their financial activities. Some groups, however, managed to survive and even evolve. These groups exhibited a range of characteristics, including lending practices, repayment policies, and meeting agendas. Group sizes also varied. Some member-owned-and-operated organizations reach membership levels in the hundreds, while others consist of no more than thirty members.

The significant achievements of many groups suggest that community-managed funds can play an important role in villages, particularly those in difficult to reach areas with very poor inhabitants. However, this article also highlights the difficulties that arise when procedures are not clear, simple, and transparent, and when all members do not have the same understanding of group objectives.

## Background

The Northern Areas of Pakistan sit at the junction of the world's three highest mountain ranges: the Himalaya, the Karakoram, and the Hindu Kush. Familiar to any serious mountaineer, this "roof of the world"—bordering Afghanistan to the north, China to the northwest, and Kashmir to the east—offers breathtaking views of distant valleys and the tallest peaks on earth. Each of the area's distinct regions has a unique culture and language, separated from one another by a jagged landscape. The famed Hunza Valley—the inspiration for James Hilton's mythical Shangri-la—is alone home to three distinct languages.

Life for the 1.3 million inhabitants of Gilgit and Baltistan, two administrative districts in the Northern Areas, is harsh. Most villagers are largely cut off from the rest of Pakistan, though the Karakoram Highway has helped to heal this cut. Built in the 1970s, the highway bevels its way into the steepest slopes, connecting rural villages to one another and to the rest of Pakistan. Nevertheless, heavy snowfall and frigid temperatures isolate the area during winter months, saddling residents with inhospitable farming landscapes and limited access to labor and financial markets.

When the AKRSP started its work in the region, per capita income was only one-third of the national average, in a generally poverty-stricken Pakistan. AKRSP is a local NGO established by The Aga Khan Foundation, Pakistan. AKRSP is one of many rural support programs founded by the foundation under the umbrella of the Aga Khan Development Network, a group of development agencies spearheaded by the spiritual leader of the Ismailis, His Highness the Aga Khan. Although one-third of the Northern Areas' population is Ismaili, AKRSP is nondenominational and works with all of the Northern Areas' diverse religious and linguistic communities.

In 1982, AKRSP began piloting a participatory development model to mitigate persistent poverty in the Karakoram. Pioneered by Dr. Akhter Hameed Khan and Shoaib Sultan Khan, the formation of community organizations promoted "endogenous and self-sustaining development" at the grassroots level.[2] Three activities provided a foundation for the new paradigm: organizational and collective management; capital generation through regular savings and access to credit; and promotion of human capital and technical skills through education and training. In addition, AKRSP provided significant development and technical assistance—irrigation channels, hydropower units for electricity generation, and agricultural training. Project staff leveraged local knowledge, such as optimal cultivation techniques or unique irrigation strategies, and mainstreamed their use. Our study, however, focused on the savings and credit practices of AKRSP Village Organizations.

Going against best practices in microcredit and development at the time, AKRSP focused heavily on savings promotion. Group members articulated a desire for credit only with the opening of markets and the arrival of new, capital-hungry technologies.[3] Through Village Organizations and Women's Organizations, project staff encouraged rural farmers first to organize and then to save incrementally to build capital. AKRSP then provided loans to the groups, which the groups later repaid to AKRSP with interest. Participation in groups instilled a culture of savings. Group savings went to school fees, village development projects, schemes to increase agricultural output, and funds for household emergencies. Some group members accumulated significant lump sums by saving as little as $0.12 every two weeks. As one group member explained: "We gather a little bit, which before had no importance to us. Children used to buy toffees and waste these amounts. But when we save in a group, our money grows slowly into a strong river." Another agreed: "We don't spend the money wastefully; it helps us during difficult times."

Groups worked like informal banks. After members deposited their savings in the group, the elected manager recorded the amount in a group register and in individual passbooks. Members deposited the total in a regulated bank, and most groups opted to earn interest on long-term (usually five-year), fixed-term deposits. Additionally, groups were able to access external loans from AKRSP, which they lent internally, enabling villagers to borrow at interest rates set by the group itself. In turn, interest at subsidized rates was paid to AKRSP for the external loans.

AKRSP adopted a "learning approach" to rural development.[4] It modified its development model on many occasions, adapting to organizational and community needs. Cognizant of the potential for misappropriation and fraud, AKRSP field accountants regularly checked groups' financial records and conducted annual audits. Group leaders were required to obtain signed permission from all members plus an AKRSP resolution to withdraw savings from the group deposit account. AKRSP staff would often visit groups to verify withdrawal claims.

## AKRSP Withdrawal and Group Sustainability

By 2001, having developed a functioning rural financial market, AKRSP terminated its savings and credit program, and a private bank specializing in microfinance was created, a first in Pakistan. AKRSP became a shareholder in the First Microfinance Bank Ltd., a bank managed by the Aga Khan Agency for Microfinance (see page 144), and contributed to its capital base. While AKRSP continued to provide significant development assistance and support for community mobilization in the villages, the First Microfinance Bank was now the direct provider of financial services.

However, the withdrawal of AKRSP from savings and credit activities may have occurred too abruptly. The First Microfinance Bank needed to cover its costs in a way the donor-funded AKRSP never did. The result was reduced access to financial services, as some groups stopped borrowing and lending once they no longer had the support of AKRSP to do so. It also took some time for the First Microfinance Bank to reach remote rural areas. In the Baltistan region, where AKRSP began working in the early 1990s after almost ten years of operating in Gilgit, many groups discontinued savings and internal lending after the somewhat abrupt cessation of external services.

Still, some groups did continue to operate, with varying degrees of success. Many groups continue to this day to hold their savings in bank accounts. As a result, the individual group members have less control over their savings, and, in many cases, groups have deposited their savings in long-term deposits and thus cannot access their savings until the term ends. Our interviews with groups and individual members showed that some groups did not really understand their deposits. Some members believed the system was effectively an individual savings account, from which they could withdraw their money as they chose. Others believed that savings were collective property intended for long-term investment, and that members could not withdraw their deposits at will. Other group members could not withdraw their savings because they did not know how. They were unaware or unsure of the proper procedures.

Though many groups have remained intact to address village development needs, and some save and lend with the First Microfinance Bank, many members are reluctant to restart group savings. They would like to access their *existing* savings before considering the idea of saving again in a group.

Social pressure may prevent individual depositors from withdrawing their savings. Aid agencies often believe that group savings is evidence of a well-organized, committed set of individuals, and groups with a solid savings balance are worthy of receiving development funds. Some Village Organizations thus "leverage" their collective savings to receive grants and projects from the government and aid agencies. This is not necessarily a bad practice, but it often reduces control by individual savers over their own savings.

Some groups, particularly those AKRSP had worked with for many years in the long-served Gilgit region, were not merely continuing to operate but were thriving. A particularly impressive example was the Shining Star women's organization. In 1994 fifteen women started with weekly savings of just $1.37 per member. Initially, group members were hesitant to borrow internally, but after a group of five women paid their loans back successfully, others began to do the same, and savers were confident their money would indeed be repaid. Today, the group has ninety-four members and has accumulated savings of over $21,960—a small fortune for any village. The entire savings is currently lent to group members at an annual interest rate of 15 percent. The resulting interest income is divided annually among members and transferred to individual member accounts.

Shining Star illustrates how effective groups understand the needs of their member communities. If a group member falls ill and needs money for medicine and cannot repay a loan, the group often decides to roll over the loan and to charge interest only. During the meetings, members often discuss more than just finance; they share problems and work together to find solutions. Some women also described how group members compete to see who can save the most.

Shining Star members credit their success to solid management practices. Decision making is transparent, and the group is audited each year by a licensed accountant in the presence of group members and religious leaders. A higher-than-average saver explained why she is confident that her money is safe: "The money comes back to me every year. The profit and everything is written in my passbook. We have proof."

Group members speak fondly of the advanced training they received from AKRSP—everything from auditing instruction to village development and agriculture training. Still, they prefer their independence to being managed or facilitated by AKRSP. Under the umbrella of AKRSP, Shining Star frequently borrowed from AKRSP to supplement the credit supplied by the group. Naturally, outside borrowing discouraged members from saving as much as possible to build up their own group fund. To make matters worse, interest income left the group with payments due to AKRSP as an external lender. Members agreed that they preferred to keep the interest income within the group and to watch the value of their savings grow. Shining Star hopes to see its success replicated by the next generation of savers. It recently initiated a new group for daughters of group members.

Ghizer 4, an eighty-two member group that has been saving and lending since 1986, has a different story. Its members report that AKRSP's withdrawal from the area limited their motivation to keep saving. Once the development projects, workshops, and audits stopped, group members began to lose interest in their savings group. The group survived and pulled itself together; members regained a sense of the importance of saving, began actively depositing regular contributions into the group fund, and began auditing its savings practices and records. Like Shining Star, Ghizer 4 believes it is stronger because it retains all interest income, and it charges higher interest rates than AKRSP previously allowed.

In addition to those groups that survived the withdrawal of AKRSP's support, new groups have spun off from old ones, and some entirely new ones have begun. The Muhammadabad group emerged in 2006 from a women's group that disbanded a few years prior. Demonstrating creative management, this group conducts loan recovery every six months—as opposed to every year, as most other groups do—and chooses its group leaders through a draw. Additionally, borrowers are required to provide two or three guarantors who promise to repay the loan in case of default. An informal village accountant audits the Muhammadabad group every year, paid by group members, and informs group members how much accumulated savings and interest they have earned. Like other groups, members save for school fees, household emergencies, and to invest in businesses. One woman borrowed to pay for her child's surgery in Islamabad, Pakistan's capital. She claimed she was able to pay back the loan easily by saving some of her husband's wages and selling extra vegetables.

Of those groups that did not survive, some disbanded because of alleged fraud after auditing by AKRSP ended. Others simply lost interest and chose not to continue saving and lending. However, even former members of the disbanded groups recall readily what they were able to achieve by organizing themselves and accumulating their own capital.

## Group Size and Dynamics

In some subregions of the Northern Areas a striking characteristic of many groups is their large size. These mostly Ismaili groups in Hunza and Gilgit reached membership levels in the hundreds. Many members preferred larger groups over smaller ones, because they lent more and therefore earned more in interest income.

Most members of a 139 person Women's Organization in Gojal we spoke with preferred sizeable groups. The tight-knit, all-Ismaili group was established in 1994 and is now self-sufficient. Its annual audits are conducted in the presence of community religious leaders. Today the group has saved US$183,000, and its assets include a collectively owned general store. The group was enthusiastic about increasing its membership. Said one member, "We want to give birth to more girls so they can join the group!"

However, large groups are not always effective. A frequent complaint is irregular attendance and the difficulty of gathering large numbers of people. For example, in Danyour, a group of twenty-five women created a separate smaller group out of a much larger one, because they were not able to attend the frequent meetings required by the original group. Some villagers maintain that in semi-urban areas, groups should be smaller because their neighbors are not as well known as in villages. Another group in Danyour said it would like a larger group in theory, but the members believe that in practice a large group would be too difficult to manage. Finally, even otherwise satisfied members of large groups complain that minority opinions can often be sidelined.

Some former members of disbanded large groups told us about lamentable incidences of "elite capture"—more influential members using group wealth and resources for personal gain. Members of a now defunct large group in Altit, Hunza, all remember the incident that pulled their group apart. The group's president convinced members to allow her to borrow twenty-five hundred dollars. One woman recalls the group's confidence in its leadership: "She told us, 'If you give me money I will triple your profit.'" The rank and file never saw that money again. The members even went to a police arbitration board and court but were not successful. Surprisingly, this same group has since reconstituted itself, but with a twist. The members save regularly but do not lend out their savings. So far, they have saved one thousand dollars.

Successful groups have tried to avoid the problem of elite capture as much as possible by following sound accounting and management rules. In some cases group leaders are required to obtain fingerprints and signatures of all group members in order to withdraw savings. The bank verifies the documents before processing withdrawal requests. Some groups have introduced guarantor systems for internal lending to ensure repayment. In general, as the groups move toward simpler and more transparent procedures and record-keeping, external audits should no longer be necessary.

## Female Empowerment and Education Promotion

When Northern Areas' Women's Organizations first formed, the group managers were often men. Today however, many women, long denied access to traditional forms of wealth and labor, control group savings and lending as well as their personal finances. We did not encounter any male-controlled women's groups. Rather, many women's groups were lending to men in their villages—and recording impressive repayment rates. Groups have also given women more respect. A married woman from Ghizer explained that she receives more respect from everyone since she joined her group: "If there is a problem, I am able to help my relatives. They respect me for it. I make my own decisions about cattle and household financial issues, and my husband and children respect me for it. Now, I respect myself."

Many of the groups in the region now recognize the importance of education for both girls and boys. Saving money for their children's long-term education is a priority, and, in the words of a group member, "not saving for just any old education—but for quality higher education, like in Abbotabad and Islamabad." In one group an elderly woman used group funds to support her son through medical school at a prestigious university in Karachi, Pakistan's commercial capital. A woman in

Ahmedabad paid for her brother-in-law's master's degree with group savings and loans. In a group in Gojal an educated daughter of one of the group members had recently returned from her schooling in Rawalpindi. Her education was supported by group funds. Anecdotal evidence reveals that educated relatives who have benefited from group funds continue to send remittances home; they thus start to educate a new generation.

## Conclusion

In just thirty years the villagers of the Northern Areas have achieved a great deal in one of the most isolated areas of the world. They have completed over two thousand construction projects, including irrigation channels and roads, provided thousands of small productive loans, increased literacy rates, and increased per capita incomes by more than 300 percent since 1982. In the words of one group member, "We were like sleeping giants before AKRSP woke us up."

Our study showed that group members themselves came together and patiently saved their hard-earned money to help their families, children, and villages. Community-managed funds help members to increase their financial resilience and to save for the education of their children.

Still, groups reported problems relating to corruption and mismanagement that became more pronounced after AKRSP stopped support. AKRSP may not have adequately prepared fledgling groups to manage themselves after AKRSP withdrew. In some cases ignorance of how groups would operate independently hurt group morale and reduced trust in savings and lending generally. More mature groups, in contrast, were able to endure the shock.

AKRSP is now considering whether to facilitate the creation of smaller groups of up to thirty members, with highly transparent and simple record-keeping, regular distributions of group savings, no external capital, and minimal but crucial financial literacy training for group members. The goal is for the groups to operate independently of AKRSP after twelve months of training and support. AKRSP believes that the villagers themselves have the ability to manage their own community funds, and it is the role of AKRSP to help them learn to do so independently and for the long term. In doing so, community members will be able to smooth their incomes, increase their ability to send their children to school, pay for medication and health services, invest in income-generating activities, and increase their financial security.

## Notes

[1] Former manager of the AKRSP in Pakistan, Stephen F. Rasmussen, in a conversation with the authors, pointed out that while individual savings did contribute significantly to the current savings amount of over $8 million, a significant portion of the portfolio came from other sources, such as negotiated labor fees to groups paid by AKRSP for village-level development projects and one-off contributions from wealthier group members. Additionally, some group members were attracted by the unsustainable high interest rates on savings paid by banks, which were subsidized by the Pakistani government from the mid 1980s until about 2000.

[2] Shoaib Sultan Khan, Hussain Wali Khan, and Khalees Tetlay, "Village Organization Banking: A Status Report as of December 1990," AKRSP Internal Report (1991).

[3] Ibid., 2.

[4] Ibid., 23.

Chapter 17

# A Snapshot of Oxfam's Saving for Change Program in El Salvador

ELOISA DEVIETTI AND JANINA MATUSZESKI

## Introduction

Saving for Change is a group savings program developed by Oxfam America in partnership with Freedom from Hunger. First implemented in Mali in 2005, Saving for Change has since expanded to Cambodia, Senegal, and Burkina Faso. In 2007, Oxfam started the Saving for Change program in El Salvador, and that experience is the focus of this chapter.

Within El Salvador, Oxfam selected the mountainous administrative region of Chalatenango as an appropriate place to begin. Chalatenango offered a remote, rural location with several strong local organizations with whom Oxfam could partner. A feasibility study carried out in August 2006 identified several additional reasons that Chalatenango would be a good location for a new informal savings program: low levels of formal employment in the local economy, high poverty rates (54 percent of the population), and no access to financial services. Despite this lack of financial infrastructure, there were some women-owned microenterprises, mostly dedicated to selling food such as tamales, cakes, pupusas (stuffed flat-bread biscuits), or farm products such as chickens. An important challenge was the absence of traditional ROSCAs; their existence in Mali and Senegal facilitated the spread of Saving for Change in those countries.

167

The 2006 feasibility study was followed by a pilot phase of the program, running from April 2007 until December 2007. Oxfam selected two partner organizations, Caritas and CCR (Asociación de Comunidades para el Desarrollo de Chalatenango), and trained them in Saving for Change practices. The partners then hired three local women as *promotoras*, local organizers responsible for starting and training groups. This small group of women eventually trained twenty pilot groups, nineteen of which are still in operation. A pilot evaluation showed that the project was functioning well, and that women appreciated the solidarity, accumulated savings, and convenient access to loans resulting from group membership. A scaled-up implementation phase began in January 2008.

Ultimately, the program hopes to reach 6,600 women by 2010. This November 2008 study evaluated the program's operational issues with a special focus on expansion. The study also highlighted some interesting findings in terms of efficacy and impact.

Ten groups were chosen to represent the 144 groups existing at the time. Five groups were randomly selected from key categories: groups in large towns, mature and new groups in remote rural areas, and mature and new groups in villages near towns or main roads. Five additional savings groups in these communities were also interviewed. The team conducted over forty individual interviews with group members, relatives of members, and non-members. The researchers spoke with local community leaders, Oxfam staff, partner staff, and *promotoras*. A mixed-method research approach involving both open-ended qualitative questions and specific quantitative questions allowed for comparisons of income, assets, and other factors across members and non-members.

## Key Findings

The study found that the program was generally functioning well; however, it did identify areas for improvement. The findings below reflect the strengths and challenges of the program in November 2008.

*Relationships with partners*

Choosing high-quality partner organizations, working with these organizations as equals, and creating a culture of open communication are crucial elements for any good development program. This is no less true for Saving for Change in El Salvador. Oxfam has worked closely with both Caritas and CCR, facilitating an open exchange of ideas and mutual respect. Three elements in particular created a productive relationship:

- *Communication:* Oxfam staff, partner staff, and *promotoras* were doing a good job of communicating openly about challenges and successes.
- *Flexibility:* Flexibility allows the program to adapt to local circumstances and to achieve both partner and Oxfam program goals. Oxfam has established the goal of incorporating local experiments and variations on its model, while still retaining the model's non-negotiable, core elements. Both Oxfam and the partners demonstrated a commitment to the evolution of the model to meet the needs of group members in the Salvadoran context.
- *Intensive support:* Oxfam staff was more involved in the El Salvador program than in other country programs, particularly in the areas of technical support and staff supervision. Expansion challenges, such as local mistrust of group structures, low levels of economic activity, inexperience with financial transactions, and the need for ongoing adaptation of this relatively new program, prompted the direct and extensive involvement of Oxfam staff.

*Program expansion and quality*

The study revealed program expansion to be one of the most complicated aspects of successful implementation in El Salvador. *Promotoras* specifically identified program promotion and recruitment as the most difficult and labor intensive parts of their job. Years of civil war and the ensuing mistrust of group associations were persistent barriers to new group formation. Additionally, a culture of dependency on NGOs had created a situation where people expected cash or in-kind handouts for participating in development projects. *Promotoras* also faced the challenge of women's minimal experience with financial services and the poverty of households, which leads many potential members to think that it is impossible to save. *Promotoras* must work hard to convince women to try the program, but once women join, they find that savings are possible after all.

The *promotoras* described the ways in which they promoted the program, from community meetings to door-to-door visits. They reported that their success relied mainly on their personal recognition and reputation in a particular community. Older *promotoras*, who commanded the respect of residents, were generally more successful at forming groups than their younger, more technically adept colleagues. Some *promotoras* devised a collaborative structure in which an older individual formed new groups while the younger *promotora* trained them. Oxfam America encouraged this initiative but stressed the importance of ongoing refresher courses for all *promotoras*. To aid with program promotion, partner staff were encouraged to attend additional community meetings to share program information and legitimize the *promotoras'* work in the eyes of community leaders.

On a structural level the study revealed the possibility that the ongoing involvement of the *promotoras* with existing groups might have hindered expansion. While *promotoras'* recruitment duties proved time consuming, no group had yet graduated to self-sufficiency, and this represented a continuing burden on *promotoras'* time and attention. Group graduation was thus critical to subsequent phases of expansion; graduated groups can function with little or no support from their *promotora*, freeing her to form and support new groups.

According to the research findings the ability to graduate a group depended on group skills and capabilities acquired during the training period: Did the group have good dispute resolution mechanisms, effective decision-making procedures, reliable and consistent leadership, and a spirit of self-reliance?

In terms of quality, record-keeping emerged as especially important to group self-management. Although members generally trusted the record keeping, only three of the ten groups were confident that they could carry out the task without ongoing assistance. In part as a response to preliminary versions of this report, Oxfam staff subsequently introduced a simplified record-keeping system and gave supplementary record-keeping training to *promotoras*.

Lending levels were another area by which the study sought to evaluate quality. Although members declared themselves comfortable with internal lending levels, these levels are low compared to other countries' Saving for Change programs. On average, only 33 percent of the total group fund was on loan. This was partly due to limited economic opportunities and to women's inexperience with starting and running small businesses, making them less willing to take the financial risks associated with a loan.

Group members, *promotoras*, and Oxfam staff all recognized the need for training on the design and management of a microenterprise, specifically training focused on product pricing and sales. This training could boost women's confidence in their ability to repay loans and potentially increase lending activity within the groups. Furthermore, if groups were to better understand the implications of different financial choices, they might make better strategic decisions that could increase the size of the collective fund.

### Financial and social impacts

The study found that Saving for Change has inspired important social changes, especially along gender dimensions, but has produced few improvements in the economic status of members. However, because of methodological challenges, specifically the lack of baseline data and a control group for this study, these results are preliminary.

Group members and non-members in the community did not differ to a statistically significant degree in terms of wealth, and members did not report significant changes in income as a result of group participation. However, without baseline data it was impossible to distinguish the initial economic status of women who were likely to join a Saving for Change group from any increase in their wealth that might result from membership.[1]

There is some evidence that Saving for Change increased members' business activities; 25 percent of members had started their own businesses since joining a group (compared to 15 percent of non-members).[2] Other women expressed interest in doing so, suggesting the possible creation of more businesses in the future. Nonetheless, because of their financial inexperience, many women focused their efforts on the immediate need to generate savings and not on long-term income-generation strategies.

The reported social effects from Saving for Change were widespread and positive, but again, these findings are preliminary. Although individuals hesitated to discuss specific experiences, many *promotoras* and group members were willing to speak in general terms about gender issues. Female *promotoras* appreciated that their role in the program helped them to expand away from their gender-defined duties of cooking, cleaning, and taking care of their families. Members reported greater self-confidence and willingness to speak in front of others since joining the program. They also described their delight in the camaraderie they had developed with fellow group members. Many women appreciated their new financial and leadership skills. Overall, women's increased self-confidence and social connections were an indication that Saving for Change is empowering women and facilitating increased social capital. Overall, one in four women members felt she had *more* authority within her family as a result of participation in the Saving for Change program.[3]

Interviews with *promotoras*, community leaders, Oxfam staff, and savings groups revealed that a number of non-members either were unable to join the program or were forced to leave because their husbands or families disapproved. The extent of this unintended exclusion was unclear. The topic of full community participation merits further attention, as it may have bearing on issues of general program expansion, as well as the inclusion of poorer or more marginalized members of the community.

## Conclusions

The operational and impact findings in this study represent an initial effort to understand the challenges and opportunities present in the region. Oxfam America hopes that these and future findings will inform expansion and help define a model to bring Saving for Change to other countries in Latin America.

## Notes

[1] For example, it could be that Saving for Change attracted poor women whose income then grew until it matched the income of those who did not join. In the absence of baseline data, this is impossible to know.

[2] Non-members were also asked if they had started a business in the previous year.

[3] Interestingly, the research team found that, even before joining the program, members were more likely to have had a higher level of decision-making capacity and autonomy over their own actions as compared to women who did not join. Women members with considerable autonomy even before the program included single women and those with absent husbands or understanding families.

Doris Dvube, a savings-group member in Nzameya, Swaziland,
explains her personal savings-and-lending plan
to fellow group members.

# PART 5

# AN ALTERNATIVE, OR SOMETHING ALTOGETHER DIFFERENT?

Savings-group promotion is still a new approach to development assistance, very much junior to the kind of microfinance supplied by banks and microcredit institutions. This section comprises four chapters that look ahead to the future of what is yet to become a movement, but is certainly beyond the stage of mere experiment.

Jeffrey Ashe is one of the founding fathers of donor assistance for financial services and indeed for microenterprise in general. He has more recently become heavily engaged in the promotion of savings groups, in particular through Oxfam America's Saving for Change program. His paper describes his personal journey since 1980, especially the results of Oxfam America's savings group experience in Mali, with which he has been very closely identified. He outlines the pluses and minuses of the approach and looks beyond the present to likely future developments.

Hugh Allen, another founding father, known for his work at CARE and particularly with Village Savings and Loan Associations, discusses in Chapter 19 whether savings groups should or should not be linked to banks or other formal financial institutions. The Srinivasan article in Part 2 discussed the Indian experience of linking groups for credit, and the Ahmed article in Part 3 described the development of First MicroFinance Bank's savings groups in Pakistan. Allen points out, however, that many pitfalls can arise from such linkages, at least from linkages where groups receive more credit, as opposed to more savings services. Savings groups can be seen either as a substitute or a preparation for institutional microfinance. Allen generally inclines to the former.

In Chapter 20 Paul Rippey picks up the issue of cost reduction. Group promotion is already very cheap, at perhaps twenty dollars a member, and this is much lower than the cost per "beneficiary" of most microfinance start-ups or other programs. His chapter points out, however, that these are undemanding standards. Donors need to spend their money, and international NGOs need to cover their expensive overheads. However, the cost of savings-group promotion should be compared with local costs for primary education or other necessities, and every possible avenue should be explored to get the costs down. Only then will it be possible to reach all the people who can benefit from membership.

Kim Wilson, Malcolm Harper, and Matthew Griffith conclude Part 5 by wondering if a focus on the financial services of savings groups is not misplaced. While members may save and borrow through their groups, these benefits seem insignificant when compared to the social paybacks that accrue over time. In India, groups have been saving for years—and breaking many of the rules held dear by experts. Groups do not use talismanic lockboxes. Nor do they predictably distribute funds back to members. Loan maturities might extend well beyond a year. Books can be messy, incomplete or incomprehensible. Yet members remain in these groups. They do so because they continue to receive social rewards that are polished, amplified, and made better with each passing year.

# Chapter 18

# The Savings-Led Revolution

*Mass-Scale, Group-Managed Microfinance for the Rural Poor*

JEFFREY ASHE

## Savings-led Microfinance

Can the poor save? Must financial services be delivered through financial institutions? When are subsidies justified? What is the best way to deliver financial services to the rural poor? What are the pitfalls? How can a workable, simple program be undercut by well-meaning agencies and donors? Why should donors fund the expansion of basic savings and lending services to the rural poor? These are the issues that will be addressed in this chapter.

In 1980 the PISCES Project[1] scoured fourteen countries and found a handful of projects with two thousand borrowers. Now, according to the 2009 *Microcredit Summit Report,*[2] microfinance institutions worldwide reach 133 million clients, a solid outcome for thirty years of hard work. But what of the half billion or more who still lack access to financial services?

Although microfinance institutions are deepening their outreach and cell-phone banking is directing services down-market in a few countries, a highly decentralized, noninstitutional, under-the-regulatory-radar, savings-led alternative approach to microfinance is showing great promise. Savings-led microfinance reaches those left out, principally the rural poor. Instead of providing financial services directly through financial institutions,

177

savings-led microfinance organizations facilitate the training of thousands of fifteen to thirty member self-managed savings and lending groups. Members save and lend to one another at interest and share the profits, much like credit unions, but at "nano" scale. Good performance depends on social pressure rather than government regulators.

The approach is simple. Since the group fund is financed entirely by tapping the under-utilized savings potential of the group members, there is no external loan fund to manage. Groups operate independently after approximately twelve months of training, and they survive even after the NGO that trained them has left (although an NGO may stay to provide other services).[3] The cost per client, typically about twenty-five dollars, is a small fraction of the per client start-up costs of a microfinance institution, and savings-led microfinance also reaches far deeper into rural areas and includes a higher percentage of the poor and very poor as clients than do microfinance institutions. As of August 2009 the major international NGOs with savings-led programs reached 1.5 million villagers in Africa, 1.2 million in Asia, and 5,500 in Latin America, with this number increasing rapidly.[4] Although microfinance institutions can provide a greater range of services, savings groups are a viable alternative for the vast number unlikely to be served by "bricks and mortar" financial institutions.

We microfinance practitioners and service providers have learned that villagers are not "too poor to save." If we had not been so focused on lending and had asked our clients, we would have quickly learned that, although they save in several mostly informal ways, the value of their savings erodes, often substantially. Under-the-mattress savings are spent, jewelry loses value when everyone is cashing in, and animals must be cared for, may die, or may not be worth much when times are hard. The issue is not the desire or ability to save but the poor quality of the savings options available.[5]

ROSCAs—called tontines, merry-go-rounds, *susus*, partners, chit funds, *tandas*, and hundreds of other local names—are often the best available savings option. ROSCAs collect an agreed-upon payment from members and pay the amount collected to each member in turn. But there are limitations: money is often not available when it is needed or in the amount needed; and malfeasance is sometimes an issue, especially when ROSCAs are large and members do not know one another well. In addition, ROSCAS are not for everyone. In many countries most of those who are part of ROSCAs are slightly better-off market vendors or employees with a steady source of income.

The principal savings-led programs—Village Savings and Loan Associations (CARE), Saving for Change (Oxfam America/Freedom from Hunger), WORTH (Pact), Savings and Internal Lending Communities (CRS), Community Based Savings Groups (Aga Khan Foundation), and self-help groups in India—are based on pooling savings in a common fund. ROSCAs become ASCAs (accumulating savings and credit associations). The difference is that loans are available when members need them, in the amount they request. Elected officers, standardized procedures, and locked cash boxes (with one person keeping the key and another keeping the locked box) ensure transparency. Not much can go seriously wrong if transactions are carried out in front of the members.

Member savings plus interest are returned to each member at the end of the yearly cycle, often just before planting, when money is scarce. It is used to purchase food, seeds, or other investments until members can enjoy the harvest. Since the interest charged on loans is paid to the group instead of an external lender, members see an annualized return on their savings ranging from 20 to 50 percent. When the first group in a village divides earnings at the end of the cycle and the others see how much they earned, new groups spring up quickly.

A major advantage to savings-led programs is that they can be carried out by the many competent NGOs already providing health, literacy, or agricultural services. The infrastructure needed to promote savings-led programs is already largely in place; there is no need to create a new delivery structure. And the model is virtually fraud proof. The NGO staff never touches the money, and since the money belongs to the members, they are careful about how their money is managed. As a group member in Mali commented to me, "The fact that the animator [NGO field staff] did not put his hand on the money is proof that the program is a matter of the women themselves."

In India many thousands of NGOs have trained self-help groups since the first groups were created twenty-five years ago. The same could be true of Africa, Asia, and Latin America in the decades to come.

## Saving for Change

One of the largest savings-led programs is the Saving for Change program promoted by my organization, Oxfam America, and Freedom from Hunger. The first Saving for Change group was trained in Mali in April 2005. The program is now operating in Mali, Cambodia, Senegal, and El Salvador, funded through foundations and private donors. After fifty months of operations, Saving for Change has grown to 291,625 members organized into 14,671 groups, with this number projected to double over the next two years. As of June 2009 the combination of interest income, savings deposits, fines on late deposits or payments, and money earned from group projects supplied $4.6 million of capital to lend to group members—an average of $315 per group with older groups managing $500, $1,000, and even more. Demand for loans is high, with 81 percent of the group fund on loan in Mali and 97 percent in Cambodia.

Saving for Change has incorporated the strongest elements of the pioneering savings-led programs, including those from Pact in Nepal, Catholic Relief Services in India, and CARE in Zimbabwe, into its initial design, and the model has evolved substantially since then. Freedom from Hunger has been our partner in this venture from the start. We built Freedom from Hunger's highly participatory "dialogue education" methodology into the training of the groups. We also built on Freedom from Hunger's expertise in training to develop a cadre of staff capable of rolling out a program with consistent quality on a national scale.

## Saving for Change in Mali

Mali is one of the world's poorest countries, and within Mali, Saving for Change reaches villages far from paved roads, indeed from any roads at all. As of June 2009 the program had expanded to 189,000 members organized into 8,310 savings and lending groups in some 2,800 villages. Virtually all members are women. The average group member is an illiterate, middle-aged woman with five children who lives several kilometers from a market and who must ration what she and her children eat while waiting for the next harvest. She is hardly a candidate for a microfinance loan. According to a survey using FINCA International's FCAT poverty assessment tool, 95 percent of Saving for Change group members earn less than one dollar a day.[6]

Given the high rate of illiteracy, the first challenge was group record keeping; most groups lacked a single literate member. Oxfam America's response was to develop an oral record system based on mental recall. The system works because each member is responsible for remembering only four facts: (1) whether or not the member made a deposit at the last meeting, (2) the amount and due date of her outstanding loan, (3) the verification of the savings and loan information of the woman sitting to her right, to ensure information was reported accurately, and (4) the amount in the box after the money was counted and the box was closed and locked. The outstanding loan balance for the group is kept by counting sticks, seeds, and pebbles. Oral record keeping has proved to be much faster and far more accurate than the poorly maintained written records, kept by barely literate secretaries, typical of many programs. The limitation of the oral system is that every member must save the same amount each week, although members with more money to deposit can opt to save multiples of the base savings amount. When the fund is divided at the end of the predetermined period, those with more savings receive a greater share of the distribution.

The Village Savings and Loan Associations (CARE) and Savings and Internal Lending Communities (Catholic Relief Services) have a different solution to the record-keeping problem. These programs use a passbook with stamps to track how much each member saves each meeting. Each stamp is a multiple of the agreed-upon base savings amount. For example, if the base savings amount is twenty-five cents and the member saved one dollar, there would be four stamps in the member's passbooks. This permits the members to save what they can every week. Drawing on these practices, in countries where the literacy level is sufficiently high, such as Cambodia and El Salvador, the Saving for Change groups use highly simplified ledgers so that members can save as much as they want at each meeting.

In Mali and Senegal unpaid "replicating agents" recruited from the groups do most of the training. This practice reduces costs and ensures that new groups will be trained and supported after the paid NGO group trainers are assigned to new villages. To facilitate their training, Freedom from Hunger and Oxfam developed a "pictographic manual" that illustrates each step in the group training process. By following this guide the illiterate replicating agents train groups of the same quality as those trained by paid staff. Freedom from Hunger's malaria training curriculum has also been simplified so it can be taught by the replicating agents. Saving and lending and malaria prevention and treatment are an integral part of the training the groups receive in Mali.

## Implementation

In Mali and Senegal it costs Oxfam $400,000 to underwrite the costs of a team from a local NGO to train eight hundred groups with sixteen thousand women in a region of three hundred villages over three years ($25 per member). This price tag includes both the cost of the NGO staff training and all the costs of training and supporting the NGO, monitoring and evaluation, and supervision. It works like this:

1. The team of ten animators and one coordinator from a local NGO is recruited and trained.
2. Each animator is assigned a cluster of thirty villages where he or she will introduce Saving for Change over three years.
3. During the first year the animators train one group in each of ten villages, and they recruit one to three replicating agents (depending on the size of the village), who are asked to train new groups that include all the women in the village. This policy ensures that the poorest are reached.
4. During the second and third year each animator starts groups in ten more villages while supporting the replicating agents in the villages trained earlier.

By the third year each ten-animator team is responsible for 800 groups. Of these, two hundred will have been trained by the animators and six hundred by the unpaid volunteer replicating agents. By taking responsibility for training groups early on, the replicating agents will have the skills to continue the program on their own and to expand Saving for Change within their villages and to additional villages in the region. Currently, seventeen animator teams are supporting 8,310 groups in Mali, an average of forty-nine groups per animator with 1,127 members. Each animator is responsible for twenty groups the first year, and eighty groups with 1,840 members the third year, with most of the groups trained in the first and second year already graduated and needing only to be monitored.

By following this well-defined procedure, Saving for Change has been able to expand quickly while maintaining group quality at low cost. These elements have proved crucial: careful selection of local partner organizations; joint hiring of the coordinator and animators to ensure quality; a tight management-information system to ensure quality; well-written, simple manuals; quality training and ongoing support; clear and ambitious performance expectations; and constant learning and improvement based on experience.

## Pitfalls

Saving for Change is a simple, robust, low-cost model that operates in regions and with a population that MFIs and credit unions scarcely touch. But when this model is described to newly interested parties, three "improvements" are typically proposed that threaten the functioning of the model.

*Matching funds:* The group is told that if the members save enough, their savings will be matched by a donor. The consequence is that groups save up to the amount of the match and then stop saving. Their motivation is to receive the match, not to mobilize their own savings. *The better alternative* is to work with groups to increase their savings rate and to use the funding that would have been used for the match to train more groups.

*Link the groups to MFIs:* Typically, MFIs take the groups' savings as collateral and flood the groups with more money than they can manage. Often the few who need larger loans borrow heavily, putting their group's savings at risk. Within the groups, compounding interest is a major driver of the growth of the group fund. If groups borrow from an institution, they pay interest to the institution, interest that otherwise would have accrued to the groups themselves had the groups used their savings as loan capital. *The better alternative* is to encourage the group to save more; the group fund can meet the growing needs of the members in two to four years. Before then, encourage members who need larger loans to go to MFIs as individuals.

***Pooling the funds of several groups into a common fund managed by an association of groups:*** When the funds of many groups are managed centrally, transparency breaks down because transactions are not witnessed by group members. The fund also tends to be monopolized by the few in the associations who need larger loans. *The better alternative* is to form associations as ROSCAs. Each group contributes an equal amount, and one or two groups receive the payout by lot. Associations become forums for exchanging learning among groups and platforms for additional training without the risk of losing transparency. In Mali two members from each group attend the association meeting; the association has its own officers.

## What This Adds Up To

Through their participation in their Saving for Change groups, women are investing in trading and agriculture. With more income they are less likely to go hungry between the planting and the harvest. The women can also pay school fees, purchase medicine, and buy "a little something" for their husbands and children. With more buying power and a group to support their progress, women take a larger role in the household and the community.

According to a May 2009 study of five villages carried out by the Bureau for Applied Research in Anthropology (BARA) at the University of Arizona,[7] Saving for Change is very effective in empowering women to make their own economic decisions, reaching women who would not otherwise be able to participate in microfinance. Participation in Saving for Change groups gives women more economic freedom, making them less dependent on their husbands for money. Membership also creates opportunities to reduce risks by better absorbing shocks, particularly related to health care. Being part of a group also mitigates short-term fluctuations in income. There is strong evidence, according to the researchers, that Saving for Change opens up investment opportunities for women that would have otherwise been beyond their reach. Greater economic security can lessen the need to migrate, which is particularly important for the poorest and often women-led households.

From a social perspective the BARA team reports that Saving for Change is extending women's social networks and appears to be empowering women. It has increased women's role in the community and improved confidence and leadership skills, giving participants a greater sense of their own capacity. Saving for Change has enhanced cooperation, mutual assistance, and solidarity among members and, more generally, in their communities.

Saving for Change will not eradicate poverty, but the lives of women members and their families have improved in ways that, from their perspective, are very important. Asked what they liked best, women rated solidarity and mutual assistance higher than saving and borrowing, with malaria training and business development following.

By 2012 we will know more about the impact of Saving for Change in Mali. The Bill and Melinda Gates Foundation has funded a randomized control trial study in five hundred villages with six thousand respondents. Saving for Change will be introduced to about half of the five hundred villages. The study will measure the differences in saving and lending, business development, food security, the use of health and educational services, social networks, and empowerment between the villages with Saving for Change groups and those without. The BARA team will continue its research in twelve villages along the dimensions mentioned above and explore the process by which these impacts occur.

## Using the Groups as Platforms for Further Development

Are savings and lending groups sufficient in themselves? Income smoothing, some poverty mitigation, and increased social capital are the predictable outcomes, but financial services are only one dimension of the challenges that villagers confront. A major problem in rural Mali is lack of water, and, with climate change, Mali is not only a dry country but is a drying country. It rains a few weeks per year, but the water runs off the hardened, depleted soil.

Could the groups serve as social platforms for work in water management? Could groups build dams or spread organic material so that water can soak into the ground, raise the water table, and extend the growing season? Could the groups be the first step toward "sustainable prosperity," where improved quality of the soil and a more reliable source of water make it possible to produce more for home consumption and for sale? Could the groups also become entry points for the introduction of appropriate technologies such as light-emitting diode (LED) solar-powered lighting, improved cook stoves, and drip irrigation? The twenty dollars or less that each of these innovations costs is within the typical loan sizes the group provides.

Understanding how the groups can be used as the first step in a larger development agenda is the next major area of innovation in the savings-led microfinance field. The challenge is to develop ways to introduce new components that reflect the mass scale, low cost, and self-replicating characteristics of the group training methodology.

## Getting Donors behind Savings-led Microfinance

Savings-led microfinance was an interesting idea a few years ago; now it is a proven methodology. The thirty million dollars in grants provided by the Bill and Melinda Gates Foundation to CARE, Oxfam/Freedom from Hunger, and Catholic Relief Services and the years of work these agencies and others invested are showing that savings-led microfinance is an important way to reach the rural poor at scale and low cost.

But unlike the MFIs, which can generate sufficient profits through interest to provide a return to investors, the savings-led model requires grant funding. The amount is very little compared to the billions that have been invested in MFIs but is still substantial. For example, a grant of approximately five million dollars would train groups with 200,000 members in more than two thousand villages in a poor country, with considerable regional variations. One hundred million dollars would introduce savings-led microfinance to twenty of the world's poorest countries and bring improved financial services to forty thousand villages that would be unlikely to be served by institutional lenders. By building on the growing institutional capacity of the major savings-led practitioners, this objective could be reached in five to seven years.

But these numbers reflect only the first stage of outreach. Looked at from a ten-year perspective, the five million dollar investment per country should be seen as the seed capital to encourage the further spread of savings-led services. Once a critical mass of local organizations is training groups funded through the initial investment, other NGOs and agencies will probably start training groups themselves, as will villagers who have participated in these groups. Furthermore, groups will start spontaneously as knowledge about this new methodology spreads informally through markets and as villagers travel from village to village spreading the word. The training materials developed and used earlier may be passed hand to hand, copied, or even sold. The challenge will be to understand how formal and informal expansion occurs and how it can be encouraged; this is a major topic for research.

## Conclusion

Despite the billions invested in microfinance over the past three decades, most of the poor still lack access to improved financial services. We suggest that savings-led microfinance that focuses on improving the quality of savings and lending services at the village level could serve much of this market. The savings-led practitioners have developed a sustainable model of microfinance, defined as groups operating on their own; in Mali, for example, after only four years nearly half of the more than eight thousand groups are operating independently. Still, some level of subsidy is needed to bring the methodology to a new cluster of villages.

What we savings-led practitioners offer is a methodology where the earnings—and they can be substantial—reside with those who should be making a profit from their efforts, the rural poor who join these groups. This potential for financial gains, along with the social capital generated and the use of these groups as a platform for other services, should be sufficient justification to fund the savings-led programs of a growing number of practitioners.

## Notes

[1] Jeffrey Ashe, *PISCES: Program for Investment in the Small Capital Enterprise Sector*, ACCION International, AITEC Division (Washington DC: Office of Rural Development and Development Administration, 1981).

[2] Sam Daley Harris, *The State of the Campaign Report* (Washington DC: The Microcredit Summit Campaign, 2009).

[3] See Valley Research Group and Linda Mayoux, *Women Ending Poverty, the WORTH Program in Nepal: Empowerment through Literacy, Banking, and Business 1999–2007* (Kathmandu, Nepal: Pact International, 2008).

[4] Hugh Allen, email with the author, August 2009.

[5] Daryl Collins, Jonathan Morduch, Stuart Rutherford, and Orlanda Rutven, *Portfolios of the Poor: How the World's Poor Live on Two Dollars a Day* (Princeton, NJ: Princeton University Press, 2009).

[6] Nicodeme Matabisi and Bersabeh Beyene, *Saving for Change Client Assessment Research* (Mali: Oxfam, 2007).

[7] BARA, *Operational Evaluation of Saving for Change in Mali* (Tucson: University of Arizona, 2008).

Chapter 19

# Pushing the Rich World's Debt Crisis onto the Poorest

*Why Savings Groups Should Not Rush to Borrow from Banks*

HUGH ALLEN

## Introduction

The recent enthusiasm for community-managed microfinance, of which ASCAs are the most widely known example, arises out of the fact that it has, beyond reasonable doubt, proven its usefulness. These groups provide safe, profitable, accessible, and well-adapted "entry level" financial services to people who live in remote rural areas and urban slums where formal service providers, such as banks and MFIs, find it difficult to cover their costs.

The self-help group (SHG) "movement" in India and the work of leading NGOs in Africa have shown that community-managed microfinance is received with enthusiasm and creates sustainable groups of owner-members who set their own rules and keep their own profits.

It is estimated that about two-thirds of the several millions of SHGs in India are linked to banks, almost exclusively to increase access to credit for their members. These linkages are achieved through a variety of mechanisms. Some groups are federated in order to strike deals with banks; some approach a local bank as independent entities. But the fundamental presumption is that groups are formed in order to get access to formal-sector credit, so that their members can take out bigger loans than would be possible using only their individual savings. This use of credit, in turn, is supposedly a precondition for creating economic security and local capital formation.

The general success of this "linkage" approach has led a number of agencies to assume that helping similar groups in other parts of the world to borrow from banks is desirable and can work as well as in India.

Why do I strongly disagree? I do so for four reasons.

### Reason one: Why debt?

I do not know why there is such an emphasis on borrowing and hardly any on savings, which is safer, easier to engineer, and a lot more useful. I usually ask enthusiasts who want to make it easy for poor people to get into debt about their own priorities for financial services. It is always the case that these credit boosters have a current checking account. Nearly all have a savings account, and most have access to some form of insurance for their health, life, car, and so on.

When it comes to credit, a sizeable minority will have taken out a loan to acquire a household asset, such as a refrigerator or an additional room. Rarely, however, has anyone taken out a loan to start a business or to increase business capitalization. This situation squares with Thomas Dichter's assertion that the history of credit in the West is that of financing consumption and the acquisition of household assets—not business investment.[1]

The obvious question to ask is *why* people who are economically secure are not investing in business. The answers vary but usually boil down to the belief that business is too darned risky; people do not know enough about it and would rather depend on their salaries. Thus, people who have multiple sources of income and a sizeable asset base consider it too risky to start businesses, but they have no hesitation in recommending debt-based enterprise strategies for people who know the least about it, whose economic vulnerability is much greater, and for whom the failure of an investment may be catastrophic. Simplistic enthusiasm to help people borrow more money can lead to pulling children out of school, forgoing meals, selling productive assets, or worse.

Surely the current financial crisis is a salutary lesson in the dangers of making it too easy to borrow. Several years ago in Malawi, I visited a group that offered some very funny theater, illustrating the contrast between savings-led and credit-led microfinance in terms of risk. The "silly" community-managed group provided modest but useful loans that did not threaten bankruptcy, and the "serious/professional" MFI carted off people's furniture. It would have been hilarious—and the village deserves full marks for retaining its sense of humor—if it had not actually happened. The difference between debt in the West and debt in Africa is that failed entrepreneurs in London and New York do not usually end up with nowhere to sleep, cook, and raise their children. It is a serious distinction.

### Reason two:
### Why assume the poor want to grow their enterprises?

Most of the poor who run businesses do so because they have no other choice; they tend to maximize drawings and minimize reinvestment. They limit their purchase of fixed assets and retain only sufficient working capital to finance the next day's production or trade. Their strategies tend toward diversification, rapid movement of working capital among enterprises, and minimal investment in machinery, skills, systems, and market knowledge.

Microfinance practitioners frequently suggest that these preferences are inefficient and somewhat undesirable. A "better" strategy would be to strive for bigger investments in technology, systems, market knowledge, and specialization, all of which more or less demand full-time engagement in the enterprise. These are the people who can create real jobs at lower cost than the modern sector and generate new capital, if they can get access to sufficient credit.

I do not disagree with any of this. It *is* desirable for capital and wealth to be generated by microenterprises. If access to loans is the major constraint to development of a sector, then efforts to supply these loans on a sustainable basis can only be welcome. But how many people are we talking about? Where do they live? And how do they live?

Most of the very poor simply do not have the luxury of being full-time businessmen and businesswomen, especially in rural areas where investment opportunities may be few. They, especially the women, have multiple responsibilities, only one of which is income generation. They have limited time and opportunity to invest in the acquisition of new skills and market knowledge. In addition, risk aversion thrusts these people toward very low-cost investment in a basket of economic activities, characterized by the rapid movement of working capital among very small, short-term household-based investments. These are not people who are in the least interested in taking on serious levels of debt to finance growth: *and they are in the vast majority*, well below the radar screen of most MFIs.

If business investments *are* to be made, there is a clear preference to make them from savings, or from local financial systems that are very well informed, not only about the community economy, but about their members' personal circumstances as well. In such situations, if things go wrong, members get a fair hearing. Such a dynamic turns what some people think of as a problem with community-managed microfinance—lack of privacy—into a tradable asset that facilitates better service, precisely *because each member is understood* and can frequently benefit from peer experience.

### Reason three:
### Why do people really want financial services?

This question goes back to my first point. Most of us do not use financial services to start businesses, or even to acquire household assets, although that option is nice. We use them to smooth income. I get an overdraft at the end of the month to tide me over to the next paycheck. I save against a rainy day, or to meet a predictable large expense. I pay for insurance so that I will not be bankrupted by illness or the house burning down. In other words, entrepreneurship is *way* down my list of priorities, and household money-management is right at the top. Why would we think that poor people have other priorities? Or are we just blinded by our assumptions about people wanting to invest their way out of poverty?

A recent FinScope study in Uganda[2] came up with a list of reasons why people save and why they borrow. There were absolutely no surprises as to why people save. The majority, 82 percent, reported saving for household basic needs, such as food, clothing, and health services. In addition, 70 percent said they saved for emergencies, and 35 percent said they saved to finance educational expenses. Financing a business was the reason 19 percent said they saved, and 12 percent said they did so to leave something to their children.

What *was* counter to orthodox belief was why people borrowed. Household needs and emergencies topped the list, with 61 percent borrowing to finance the former, and 32 percent borrowing to finance the latter. Another 19 percent borrowed to finance education. Only 15 percent borrowed to finance a business.

Where, I asked myself when I first saw these numbers, were all these budding entrepreneurs, this rush to get ahead? I can only conclude that *all* types of financial services are seen by the poor mainly as a way of making sure they protect their assets, pay their bills, keep their kids in school, and avoid falling by the wayside. Rather like everyone else.

What is striking is not only that the top three borrowing categories were the same as they were for savings, and had nothing to do with business, but also that more people preferred financing business through savings rather than debt. It is also noticeable that there was a higher incidence of response, by purpose category, for savings relative to credit, a finding constantly validated by the roughly two-to-one ratio of savers to borrowers in MFIs where savings are offered. This study is only one of many FinScope studies in Africa that consistently show the same purposes and preferences.

So where does this idea come from that people want bigger and bigger loans that can only happen through borrowing from banks? Mainly, I think, from a failure of imagination, empathy, and analysis. And patience.

### Reason four:
### Why do we think that outside capital is needed at all?

I am not saying that people do not want to borrow, and I do not mean to imply that the poor are not smart enough to manage more complex forms of finance. There is no doubt that community-managed financial services provide an opportunity to increase investments and enterprise activity. And they do so at a pace that accommodates the need to become incrementally more experienced as entrepreneurs.

So, at some point there *may* be a need for more capital. But it does not follow that community-managed savings groups can never generate the sort of money that will make a real difference from local savings and interest income, and must therefore borrow from outside.

I have visited dozens of groups that have significantly increased their capital base over time, even when using a time-bound methodology that calls for the distribution of all current assets every year. In Zanzibar, between 1990 and 1992, CARE started forty-three groups, with twenty-five to thirty members each, which shared out an average of fifteen hundred dollars at the end of the first year. Four years later, after CARE was long gone, the number of groups had mushroomed to about 150 and were sharing out (distributing the fund back to members) four thousand dollars.[3] In December 2008 this figure had risen to a reported six thousand dollars. I have visited five-year-old groups sitting under trees in Mozambique managing nine thousand dollars. Even in Niger, the poorest country in the world, these groups are managing between eight hundred and fifteen hundred dollars.

In other words, the money is usually enough for all but the rare individual exception, who can, very often, belong to a formal MFI as well as a community group. What makes the difference is giving these groups enough time to learn to roll over a proportion of their current assets from one cycle to the next—not rushing to indebt them because we assume they have neither the vision nor the capacity to do it on their own.

If we look at community-managed groups after just a year we conclude that everyone had a good time and the cash-out money was nice but not life changing. If we look at them five years down the line, we see a wholly different picture. It is normal for average share values to double from cycle to cycle as members become confident that the system actually works. It is also normal for loan sizes to increase dramatically, year on year, and to be repayable over a longer period of time, often leading to diversification into group-based trade—all without outside capital and without outside technical support.

If we did not consistently fall for the rhetoric that we purport to reject, that the poor cannot save and have solid capabilities, and if we were less determined to be at the "cutting edge," we might see some remarkable results, with a lot less risk and potential for pain.

## The Evidence

There is increasing interest in bank-linkage programs in Africa, but to date the evidence from agencies that have tried it is mixed at best. There have been cases where groups were flooded with external credit, with as many as 25 percent struggling to repay. Many longstanding groups have been forced into liquidation owing to predatory and irresponsible lending practices by MFIs that over-lend and fail to adapt repayment schedules to rural cash flows.[4] Where working models exist, as in Rwanda, the institutional delivery system has neither covered its costs nor elicited real enthusiasm from the banking sector—and this in the only country in Africa where there is an extensive rural banking network.[5]

I do not mean to say that the effort to facilitate bank linkages in Africa is doomed, but it is not going to be easy and will certainly be expensive. And every penny spent creating these relationships is a penny that is denied to an expansion of the basic community-managed model, missing opportunities to provide entry-level financial services to people who, presently, have none at all.

Uganda is a crowded microfinance market, yet 50 percent of people have no access to savings services of any type, and 60 percent have no access to credit. Only 4 percent of the population save with MFIs and formal savings and credit cooperatives, and only 2 percent receive credit from these sources. Meanwhile, over 30 percent receive savings services, and 33 percent receive credit, from informal sources. Surely it makes more sense to invest in extending informal services to the 50 to 60 percent who have no services at all, rather than seeking to link the 30 percent who do to allegedly superior product offerings. There is a real cost-benefit decision here that has not been carefully explored.

## If SHGs in India Are Successfully Linked to Banks, What Is My Problem?

I must preface this section by noting that I will be making general remarks about Indian SHGs, when these groups almost defy definition and operate in very different ways. I also know that SHGs are a remarkable phenomenon, and it only surprises me that so many people still think that community-managed microfinance lacks legitimacy, as if forty million people have been afflicted with simultaneous irrationality. The sheer scale and speed of change makes it hard to ignore that something is going on that poor people seem to find useful. And there is clear evidence from India that they do. But because SHGs are mainly linked to banks, it is often assumed that this is the way all community-based microfinance programs ought to be implemented worldwide. But is this necessarily the case?

The SHG model is being exported across the globe, but it has not yet been tried in many places in Africa, and—as already noted—the effort to link community-managed groups to banks is usually difficult and frequently negative. What are the conditions that make successful linkages so difficult in Africa?

First, the legal and regulatory environment is different. The government of India mandates banks to provide 40 percent of their lending to pro-poor sectors. Institutions such as the National Bank of Agriculture and Rural Development (NABARD) refinance SHG portfolios at a significant discount. And, critically, the banking infrastructure is extensive, with a branch in every three or four villages. None of the above is true in Africa.

Second, nearly all of the community-managed microfinance models used in Africa cash-out at the end of the annual cycle, but most Indian SHGs do not, in so far as we know. Cash-out is popular because it provides a useful lump sum to every member at a time of the year that is normally associated with a common expense, such as festivals, the planting season, and so on, and it significantly reduces systemic risk and complexity. Cash-out keeps things simple, and most African community-managed microfinance groups are fully independent of their parent agencies after one year or less; Indian SHGs take several years to achieve independence, if they ever do.[6]

Third, because it is expected that most SHGs will not cash out but will pay dividends and also be linked to banks, these groups normally maintain comprehensive records. Because it is usually not possible for the members to maintain these records to a standard that will satisfy a formal lender, most SHGs remain tied to parent NGOs for many years, with a lot of technical functions permanently externalized.

Finally, NGO coverage is much more extensive in India and much lower cost than in Africa. Thus, while outreach and long-term technical support may be affordable in India, although much of this is subsidized on a long-term basis, it is much less so in Africa. The tradeoff is clear: where long-term technical backup is available, more sophisticated services and systems can be delivered, and linkages to financial institutions may be successfully engineered, but at the cost of reduced group autonomy and a much higher price tag for implementing organizations and donors.

## Conclusion

What I am saying is that debt-based bank linkage is not a sine qua non for community-managed MFIs. I believe that linkage thrives under the favorable conditions that pertain to India but are absent elsewhere. My basic points are that bank linkages are not needed by most of the poor; that the question of linkages is not a simple or obvious one; that an overweening determination to pursue linkages may divert resources from providing entry-level services to a lot more people; and that linking to banks poses real risks, especially to rural community-managed groups and their savings.

I am also amazed that so quickly after being standardized and moving to scale, so many people want to change community-managed microfinance into something that is much less elegant, significantly more complicated, full of risks, and by the way, expensive.

## Notes

[1] Thomas Dichter, "The Chicken and Egg Dilemma in Microfinance: An Historical Analysis of the Sequence of Growth and Credit in the Economic Development of the 'North,'" in *What's Wrong with Microfinance*, ed. Thomas Dichter and Malcolm Harper (Rugby, Warwickshire, UK: Practical Action Publishing, 2007).

[2] FinScope Uganda, "Results of a National Survey on Access to Financial Services in Uganda Final Report" (Kampala: The Steadman Group, 2007).

[3] Ezra Anyango, Ezekiel Esipisu, Lydia Opoku, Susan Johnson, Markku Malkamaki, and Chris Mosuke, "Village Savings and Loan Associations—Experience from Zanzibar," *Small Enterprise Development* 18, no. 1 (2007): 11–24.

[4] Author's study in Niger in 2007, validated by a study by Paul Rippey, "Etude sur l'impact des crédits extérieurs sur les groupements et réseaux MMD et les mesures de minimisation des risques" (Réalisée pour CARE Niger et ses Partenaires Janvier, 2008).

[5] Jan Maes and CARE EDU, "Linkages between CARE's VS&LAs with Financial Institutions in Rwanda" (CARE, 2007).

[6] Ajay Tankha, *Self-help Groups as Financial Intermediaries in India: Cost of Promotion, Sustainability and Impact* (New Delhi, India: Se-Dhan, 2002).

Chapter 20

# More! Better! Cheaper!

*Savings Groups as Commodities*

PAUL RIPPEY

## Introduction

Leading savings-group implementers are taking significant steps to bring costs down. Organizations are simplifying systems and encouraging independent replication—existing group members themselves forming new groups. Implementers are also beginning to compare costs among programs. Still, most people would agree that as an industry, we can do better.

While the variations among groups in terms of memory-based systems, written records, variable and fixed savings contributions, insurance funds, savings-to-loan ratios, gender inclusion, platforms for other services, and so on are fascinating, they are of trivial importance compared to the core value of the groups: providing people an opportunity to save and borrow transparently and at little or no cost. As far as I am concerned, savings groups are commodities; who the supplier is, or, in this case, the promoter, is less important, as long as we can get out the product affordably and on time. Let us not forget that these groups *all* work. All the intriguing details that I enjoy discussing as much as anyone else are, fundamentally, just icing on the cake. Let us first be sure to get the biggest cake possible into the oven, so that everyone will be served.

And so the question: what would it take to get community-based savings groups everywhere? There is convincing evidence that, once established in an area, savings groups will continue. But how can we get them into every village and neighborhood where they would be useful? To obtain this kind of scale we have to face some hard facts about outreach and efficiency.

## At the Moment, How Are We Doing?

Current outreach and efficiency in the expansion of savings groups still fall short of the possibilities. Let us look at some numbers:

I worked for a large international donor in Uganda for five years, and our single biggest grant was for savings-group promotion. Our grantees were particularly successful at creating groups, and we and other donors ended up with about 120,000 members after eighteen months of hard work. Rounding off, we spent $2.5 million over a year and a half to get to this point.

How does this effort correspond to the opportunity or the need? The FinScope Uganda study found that 8.1 million adult Ugandans have no financial services whatsoever.[1] A very conservative estimate is that half of them are potential savings-group members, and many of those who are now clients of MFIs and savings and credit cooperatives might *also* profit from membership in savings groups, either in addition to, or in place of, the services they are now using. Let us say that the potential market for savings-group membership is four million Ugandans. In that case, we reached 3.75 percent of the potential market, for two and a half million dollars. To reach the entire market at that rate of spending would cost $80 million, in one country of thirty million people. We are simply not going to find that amount of subsidy, nor should we. Such a strategy would not be the best use of scarce development resources. And this is Uganda. Multiply the cost in Uganda by the African continent, and the costs are in the billions of dollars.

Or consider this: during the period of eighteen months when we trained 120,000 group members and had excellent donor and implementer coordination, Uganda's population increased by about ten times that number. That is, Uganda's population of twenty-eight million, with a 3.4 percent annual growth rate, is increasing by over 900,000 people per year.

One more thing: we are all used to saying, "Compare the cost of a new savings-group member to the cost of a new client in a MFI." This is an imperfect comparison for two reasons. First, MFIs do a terrible job of reaching downward. In fact, no institution serves the population that is served by savings groups. At present, savings groups seem to be the only viable way to bring decent services to large numbers of very poor people in remote areas.

But second, and more important, it is out of date to compare savings groups to credit-only MFIs. These credit-only operations are relics of the twentieth century, and fortunately, they are rapidly being replaced by more sophisticated institutions. Credit-only MFIs are too easy a target. Let us be tougher on ourselves and compare savings-group costs and outreach to those of institutions like Equity Bank, Afriland Bank, and Centenary Bank, which are among the African financial institutions of the future.

Two years ago Equity Bank added a million accounts in about twelve months with no donor operating subsidy, and it is providing excellent outreach and depth that may soon be within shouting distance of the savings-group market. A million clients at zero dollars each of donor funding: now, *that's* efficiency. Of course, Equity's clients are not quite the poor women sitting under the mango tree who belong to savings groups. Nonetheless, we should not feel superior to well-run financial institutions simply because we can incorporate new members into savings groups for twenty dollars a head.

Also, technology will surely come down to the savings-group level, sooner or later. Mobile banking is still too expensive for many savings-group members, if it is available at all. But someday soon it might be cheaper to buy poor people phones that they can use to facilitate savings and borrowing activities than to spend twenty dollars training them in a savings-group approach. In the long run, technology usually wins.

Frankly, our assessment of costs betrays our donor orientation. Twenty dollars per member might be inexpensive compared to usual NGO cost per beneficiary, but let us use a different standard: Ethiopia spends less than ten dollars per student annually on primary education; few if any sub-Saharan countries spend as much as one hundred dollars. No one thinks African primary education is a resounding success. However, in most countries it represents a sincere attempt at inclusion, with ambitious goals bumping into severe resource constraints and growing pains.

Perhaps the quality of services in savings-group programs is better than the quality of services in most school systems. However, national governments cannot afford to be elitist. Education ministries have a mandate to reach everyone, while we are reaching a tiny percentage of our market and not even keeping pace with population growth. In terms of ambition and outreach, I have to award the victory wreath to the schools; they are aiming much higher than we are, and they offer a year of a child's schooling for the same price that we offer a few training sessions to adults in procedures that we keep insisting, correctly, are easy to master.

Also, while I am always cheerfully ready to criticize MFIs, let us not ignore their strengths, one of which is communicating simple messages effectively to large numbers of people. Of course, most microfinance training is simply training in loan repayment, achieved through a mix of information, threats, admonition, inspiring examples, anecdotes, lies, and evocations of religion and local tradition.

Even if the practice is not always noble, it is usually efficient. When I worked with Al Amana in Morocco, I used to watch groups of new clients lining up to go through the indoctrination in loan repayment that our agents provided. Our incentive system for the credit agents meant that they could double or even triple their salaries by training large numbers of people well. They got very, very good at it. Even a non-Arabic speaker like myself could see the friendly welcoming smiles alternating with dramatic flourishes, the eye contact, the frequent stops to have the clients repeat what had just been said, and the suspenseful pauses as they waited for each potential borrower to commit himself or herself to one hundred percent respect of procedures.

The best agents had acolytes who would come to sit at the feet of the masters and learn their training techniques. As they got more effective, they also got more efficient. We had originally planned three one-hour sessions for clients before giving them loans. The best agents reduced the hour to forty-five minutes or less, and sometimes combined sessions. At the management level we often did not know about these shortcuts, and we certainly did not care, as long as the results were good, which they almost always were.

However, with savings groups one does not usually see the same incentives for high productivity. Community-based trainers—people from local communities charged with replicating savings groups—sometimes carry out thirty or forty visits to a group in the first year. Despite what we say about graduation, trainers often stick with the group after it had made its distribution, even when the group has clearly mastered everything it needs to know. I have often asked trainers and groups why the trainer is still coming to meetings, when the group seems to be carrying out its business quite well, thank you. "Well, they are doing a good job, but . . . they still need me," is a typical trainer response. The group says, "Well, we are fine, and we would do this just the same without the trainer, but . . . we still need her." This co-dependence seems to come from the desire of the group to have a continued window to the outside world through the implementing organization, and the desire of the implementing organization to have continued access to the groups. Fair enough. But this is not an efficient way to increase outreach. Someone else should pay for superfluous visits, not the donors trying to buy outreach.

The evaluation of savings-group experience in Zanzibar[2] showed that many groups were not getting "enough" training and yet were functioning perfectly well. That conclusion seems to indicate two things: the model is robust, that is, if you get it more or less right, it still works; and we overestimate the amount of training needed.

Now, what about situations where there are clear problems with group mastery of basic concepts? I have seen plenty of groups that were quite shaky in their understanding of the rules, or which were burdened by complicated record-keeping systems that they were far from mastering, or groups that had invented modifications which experience elsewhere suggested would not work in the long run. I think it is highly likely that the problem in these cases lies not with the amount of training but with its quality. In fact, some of the worst groups I ever saw—in Arua, Uganda—had received three years of regular visits and still had not mastered some of the most basic principles. Running a savings group is a simple task. If groups have been presented with the curriculum and still do not get it right, the problem is not in the number of training hours but in the quality of that training.

In fact, it is likely that giving groups large or indefinite numbers of training sessions will create more problems than benefits. Excessive training builds dependency, undercuts independence and self-reliance, delegates problem solving to outsiders, and is likely to lead the trainer to add unnecessary and complex bells and whistles to the system. A limited training budget will challenge creative trainers to innovate in terms of efficiency instead of complexity. The hardest thing about savings groups is keeping them simple.

We have only begun to think about efficiency in training techniques, and I suspect there is a lack of demand for efficiency and mastery at many different levels of the system. At the risk of offending almost everyone, I have to say that the savings-group enterprise reflects its existence in the nonprofit sector and not in the for-profit sector. Donors do not demand enough of their grantees. Grantees do not demand enough of their implementing partners. Partners, in turn, are too relaxed with the community-based trainers. And trainers do not project the demand for mastery that is a necessary element of effective training.

The best MFIs keep reducing their interest rates as they grow, because they capture so many economies of scale. Two of these that I know fairly well, Al Amana in Morocco and Equity in Kenya, have continued to reduce their costs while their profits continue to rise. However, economies of scale do not fall from the sky. One has to fight for them. Management needs to take hard decisions, including human-resource decisions. Information and communication technology needs to play a larger role. Product design and pricing need to be scientific. Some of the best local MFIs have had consultants sit in the banking hall, surreptitiously timing the average transaction time at the teller windows and working with management to shave off a few seconds here and there. What corresponds to that drive for efficiency within our savings-group programs? How much efficiency, measured in cost per member, are we gaining as we move from one thousand to ten thousand members, or one hundred thousand to a million?

## Thoughts on the Way Forward

So, how to get more efficient? Mainly, we must seriously and systematically *learn from one another*. Here are some examples:

First, *work is easier with the right tools*. It is quite remarkable that many programs try to train rural people *without* pictures or other teaching aids, which are common in health, literacy, and agriculture training. Let us find out the best low-cost tools to give to community-based trainers.

Next, *let the members do some of the work*. If the results that some programs seem to be getting with independent or viral replication are as good as they look, it would be unconscionable for other programs not to borrow that approach. Enough said.

In Zanzibar, I saw two groups, an experienced group and a new one, meet together. In perfect discipline the new group (of men) watched the older group (women) carry out a meeting. Then the newer group held its meeting and the older group watched. Then there was a short period for observations, and the groups went their way. That was the best savings-group training I have ever seen.

Third, *keep it simple*. Groups function perfectly well without ledgers. Now, many groups still want to keep some kind of centralized records. But, that is their responsibility, not ours. The fact that groups like ledgers is not a reason to spend scarce resources in training them in their use. I suspect that keeping centralized ledgers can double the time required to train a group. Drop 'em, I say.

Fourth, let us *get serious about personnel costs*. There is a huge divergence in what trainers earn in different countries and programs, and in the levels and cost of support and management staff. In Uganda we funded multiple levels of staffing in international NGOs and multiple levels within a dozen local partners. This simply cannot be the most efficient approach, and funding will eventually find efficiency.

Fifth, let us all buy into an *efficiency-oriented research agenda*. The randomized control group tests that are being carried out now should tell us something about impact; to find out about efficiency, on the other hand, programs can simply experiment and record results with different service delivery models.

A principal determinant of the cost of group formation is the *number of contacts* between community-based trainers and groups. Let us do some tests in which we reduce those contacts toward the breaking point, and then back off a bit. Does anyone think we need more than thirty contacts to train adults? Okay, you do that, and record the results. How about twenty? Ten? Seven? How about an all-day training session once a month, instead of weekly sessions? How about training multiple groups at once? If we adjust the incentive systems so they reward trainers for getting the message across, instead of prescribing the number of training sessions, the thousands of trainers around the world will come up with some breakthroughs in efficiency that we never would have thought up. We should never underestimate the collective intelligence of large numbers of motivated people.

Let us invest a bit to *learn what other disciplines already know* about training of trainers and adult education. There is a huge literature in health and agriculture, and much local experience.

Finally, let us recognize the value of *competition and incentives*. Donors should not hesitate to fund multiple grantees in the same geographical area and see who can get the most production the most efficiently. We should continue and intensify cross-country and cross-program comparisons. We should encourage implementing partners to switch from fixed salaries to incentive systems for community-based trainers. Efforts now under way to standardize the calculation of "cost per member" should be a huge step forward.

## Notes

[1] See the finscope.co.za website.

[2] Ezra Anyango, Ezekiel Esipisu, Lydia Opoku, Susan Johnson, Markku Malkamaki and Chris Mosuke, "Village Savings and Loan Associations—Experience from Zanzibar," *Small Enterprise Development* 18, no. 1 (2007): 11–24.

# Chapter 21

# The Box and the Ark

KIM WILSON, MALCOLM HARPER,
AND MATTHEW GRIFFITH

## Untold Stories

Choose your country—Cameroon, Nepal, Egypt—and you might hear cash shuffling from hand to hand and coins falling into crude vaults of tin, clay, or wood. You might hear singing as members count their annual savings, or the thrum of applause as they cheer a new loan taken or deposit made.

There is a sound we are not hearing. It is a cry of pain in the night as a man punches his wife, or the thud of police as they round up unlucky villagers, charged with crimes they never committed. It is the grunts and groans of unwanted men on top of girls, their mothers turning a deaf ear because they do not feel they have a choice.

Eventually, these mothers might join a savings group. They grow tired of the punches and the thuds. They want a better life for their daughters. Yes, they want money, but money is often the least of what they want. They want the support of other women and men.

To show what we mean, let us turn to an unpublished book on savings groups in India. Several local organizations in that country compiled stories reported by group members. The product, the book itself, though intended at one point for fundraising purposes, was never used to raise funds: the drawings were too graphic and the stories too long and harrowing.

To produce the narratives, the organizations ushered hundreds of men and women though a series of workshops. Some came to listen, and others to tell stories. Each storyteller was assigned a reporting team. The team included a scribe, who recorded the narrative; an editor, who verified it; and a local artist, who illustrated it. According to workshop rules, the reporting team could not begin to document a new storyteller until the current one had agreed that her narrative and accompanying drawings were perfect. The process of logging the history of a single participant lasted hours, and the entire process of recording, illustrating, and editing the full anthology required months.

We open the book to a scene of children picketing the home of a man who has refused to send his young daughter, Manga, to school. The story tells us that the father has married off his first daughter at the age of thirteen. The picketers, children of savings-group members, have, with their mothers' encouragement, set out to shame the farmer into sending little Manga to school. The image shows Manga behind bars as dozens of children encircle her home.

"On a Saturday morning," goes the story, "Sadhe was surprised to a see a group of sixty children in front of his house. A tiny boy ten years of age was at the forefront. The children started shouting, 'Sadhe, send your daughter to school.'" Sadhe eventually gave in to the demands of the protestors and allowed Manga to begin her education.

This child-to-adult approach quickly spread to other areas. Dedicated leaders of savings groups coached their own children to help others get the parental permission needed to attend school. The story makes no mention of savings contributions, loan amounts, interest rates, or anything at all having to do with money.

## Life Savings

Nor is money mentioned in this story about a flood in Gujarat. The illustration shows three savings-group members standing half-submerged in a raging river, holding a chunk of land above their heads. The land supports a bullock, a family, a hut, a tree, and some food. The narrative describes how savings-group members made dozens of rescues during the flood and cared for victims during the months after the waters receded.

Later in the book we glimpse more images of floods, this time in the state of Orissa. In the drawing we see several group members, all women, standing at the bow of a boat, home built and fragile looking, nosing its way through the roiling waters. The women in the sketches are rescuing neighbors from their damaged rafts, toppling rooftops, and distal branches of trees. The story explains that, as the river churns around them, these women beach their wooden boat on a patch of high ground. From a shed they bring out a great caldron and bundles of fuel stored in advance for just such an emergency. Into the cooking vessel they empty large bins of grain. The bins had been filled by the savings group during an earlier harvest, and now their rice, dhal, and black gram would become part of a warm meal for stranded children and elders.

In the more than seventy narratives contained in the collection, money is mentioned now and then, but only as a means to an end. There are drawings of groups dodging mudslides, repairing fences, and caring for children infected with AIDS. There are images of women being sprung from giant cages, and children from small cages, and groups breaking free of chains anchored down by giant cannon-balls bearing words like "insults," "communal traditions," and "discrimination." One sketch shows more than a dozen people crowded inside a glass bottle; a fat man, presumably the local landlord, is squeezed into its neck like a cork. The next image shows the bottled women shattering the glass and releasing themselves into various dream-like clouds of health, schooling, and leisure.

Curiously, or perhaps conclusively, in this story there are no illustrations of money.

## The Quest for Legibility

In savings group promotion we struggle to make our work legible. We want to gather complex, messy issues into a single optic. Thus, the groups we promote are bounded in time and in space. Obediently, members cash out once a year. Obediently, they lock and unlock their boxes while sitting in a tidy circle.

But savings groups in India defy legibility. Some last for years with no pre-established distribution of the contents of the box. Groups may never harvest the funds inside. In fact, in many places where groups gather there is no box, just a sack containing bits of cash passbooks wrapped in colorful paper.

It is easy to understand why the lockbox has become the talisman of savings-group promotion. We can count its contents—money. But counting money to find evidence of human development is like counting stars to find evidence of heaven. Money is not the only way women count success. They count the hours of help they receive from neighbors, or the evenings free of beatings by drunken husbands, or the days without the verbal abuse of employers. They count more children in school, wells in the village, flood survivors, midwives, ambulances, bicycles, and mobile phones. And more rescues of all kinds.

Let us return to the book of stories. One sketch shows a group member, Ramila, holding her children tight against her breast while a man, her father-in-law, takes a pick to the head of his son, Ramila's husband, and cleaves it. There had been a quarrel about land in the family.

Ramila, the narrative tells us, roars through the village, rallying members of her group to come to her aid. Together, they race the bleeding husband to treatment. The first clinic refuses to admit him, claiming staff cannot attend to patients who have been in a dispute. The group scrambles to find another taxi and rushes the desperate couple to a different hospital, this one even further away from the village.

Back home, Ramila's savings group takes up a collection to pay for mounting and exorbitant medical costs. Members tell Ramila that they will harvest her crop while her husband heals. As the women begin to cut the wheat, Ramila's father-in-law, the man who split her husband's head, enters the field and waves a club at the first person he sees. The brigade of harvesters, about forty strong, rises from its stooped position and encircles the father-in-law. As the men and women begin to close in on him, he flees in haste. Ramila's field is harvested.

The story goes on, like a tale from the Vedanta. Ramila's group never cashes out. It saves and lends season after season. The loans it provides are used for cows and wells, and the purchase of land—credit that requires years to repay. And throughout this journey, and thanks to the group, children are attending school, landlords are ceding power, and domestic violence is blocked time and again.

Ramila's story does not follow the arc of a Western narrative. It does not contain a start or a finish. Nor do the other stories in the book. They meander with one page elaborating the previous or one page contradicting the next. The stories entertain, comfort, and discomfit.

## The Ark, Not the Box

What is the point of these tales? Why should we care about them? They tell us something important: we should pay less attention to the box, a rustic container stamped out by practitioners, and more attention to the ark, an ampler vessel desired by members. The box limits women to rituals that we practitioners can comprehend, while the ark carries women into worlds that they would wish to dream about: protection from immediate danger or distraction from the grinding, repetitious work at home or in the field. As practitioners, we understand the ark less because we understand the fullness of women's lives less. Given the chance, we strip the ark back down to a box and tinker with its locks, hinges, and keys.

We even pronounce the funds inside the box, those funds which remain un-lent, to be idle. To us, idle funds are unproductive funds and should be disbursed as loans to generate a return. To the women members in these stories, however, the idle funds in the ark are *rashi* (wealth) and constitute financial reserve, group capability, and personal power. In one story a savings group gives its entire savings to a woman suffering a difficult childbirth. The women narrate that they are happy to have saved the lives of the mother and child. They will start saving their money for their loan fund anew.

## Kindred Savers

We writers promise never to reduce savers and borrowers to the mild, bucolic idea of a woman—a person who night and day toils for her children (though she may toil), or a wife who would take the blows of her husband (though she may take those blows), or a person who opens and shuts the cash box (though she may use a cash box).

We promise to take her stories seriously and acknowledge that her desires match ours. We want fewer burdens in our lives. So does she. We want to be shielded from looming crises. So does she.

Women want to leave behind permanently the shame of standing in labor cues or the fear of the coming floods. They do not want to be sold, married off young, or infected with disease. Neither do we. They want life to be less dreary and a lot more fun. They enjoy street theater but would prefer the entertainment of TV and radio. As would we.

We can help transform their rude boxes into bold arks. We can start with the banking function of the box. Now, the lockbox is a piggy bank. With financial technology, say a smart phone, members might pool and analyze information from savers and borrowers; the box might function as a real bank. Financial technology can reduce the chore of tedious record-keeping, or eliminate the difficult and often dangerous tasks of managing and moving cash. SIM cards and debit cards stored in the cash box will serve as a record of group transactions, show payments forwarded to a bank, or surplus funds lent to a group nearby. They will record the savings and credit history of each borrower. Someday, that history will help a member lay cash away for her daughter's college education, or purchase weather insurance, or invest in land to which she has full title.

Next, practitioners can help expand the ark beyond its limited function as a folk bank. Technology offers possibilities here as well, bringing a world of service into the hands of group members. Women will be able to use their phones or laptop computers to locate bus schedules, map the quickest route to a hospital, or find markets with better prices for their goods.

Websites like Ushahidi.com already update interested people across the world in the latest human rights violations with real-time, ground-level perspectives. A similar site might post group photos so that kindred savers across the world can meet and exchange ideas. Maps might pinpoint meeting places, clinics, and secondary schools. These websites might record births and deaths, and the legal registry of land. With smart phones and their brightly colored icons just around the bend in many rural areas, we can imagine a rich array of services widening the ark.

And let us not forget the ark as entertainment. In an effort promoted by NABARD, groups in the Indian state of Maharasthtra set portions of their money aside for a "women's drudgery fund." Different groups used this fund in different ways. Some engineered showers that piped hot water into their individual huts, which they said was most welcome at the end of a long day of planting, threshing, pounding, or grinding. Others pooled funds to go to the local cinema, and others to shop for bangles and cloth. The beauty of the Women's Drudgery Fund is that its contents are not intended for productive uses, or even emergencies. Money is meant to offer a diversion to women—diversions that they can anticipate, relish, and recall with fond memories.

Women savers have stepped out of their boxes. It is time for us to follow.

Three generations of savers in Rajasthan, India, invest their
savings and loans in water harvesting and school tuition.

# Conclusion

Anyone who has read the book this far has sampled a wide range of savings-group experiences. In fact, by the admittedly low standards of the development community, any such person might claim to be an expert in the subject.

In this final article, the editors would like to highlight what freshly minted experts should reasonably conclude, should not conclude, and what they may expect of savings groups in the future.

## What We Should Not Conclude

### We should not conclude that savings groups work

While we know that groups collect savings and make loans, we lack substantial evidence of positive financial impact on members. We do not know, for example, whether individuals increase total household savings through savings-group activities. We assume a member watches her household savings grow as her group savings grow. But, the reverse could be true. She may be watching group savings grow as her household savings shrink. To collect money needed for each group deposit, she may have buried less cash in the ground, stored less value in her assets, given fewer coins to her local savings collector, or, in places like Kenya and the Philippines, she may have stored less value in her mobile-phone account. Lacking sufficient evidence, we are unsure that money saved in a communal fund is more secure or profitable than money saved in other ways.

Nor do we know if group savings leads to increased capital for individual businesses. Common practices point to the opposite: Most promoted groups are taught to cash out every year, to draw a line under their proceedings, and to distribute

215

their accumulated fund to shareholders. This practice militates against any one member acquiring a large enough sum to fund a business. Ambitious entrepreneurs need a wide range of sources of capital, of which a savings group may be one, but not necessarily the only one, or even the most important one.

### We cannot conclude that groups are worth the price of their promotion

Even when groups are cheap to form, the cost of their monitoring can be expensive. At the very least donors must peer in on them now and then to verify their existence. Members must be counted, group attendance verified, cash reckoned, data entered, and analysis performed.

One wonders, when considering the expense of monitoring, if groups should be promoted at all. Would the installation of a solar-powered generator, a dairy-processing plant, or reclamation of a piece of land offer more "bang for the buck" than the promotion of a cluster of savings groups? We do not know, and this book is unable to answer that question.

### We may not conclude that groups should comprise only women members

Many of the NGOs and promoters described in this book emphasize women membership. Women are attractive targets for development agencies for several reasons. Development agencies believe women to be poorer than men, and therefore worth the emphasis. Agencies also believe women make better members: they are better savers (more reliable with a more natural sense of thrift); better borrowers (more likely to repay their loans); better participants (more dependable at meetings and submissive to group decisions); and better users of savings (more willing to invest in family health and education). Little hard evidence supports these beliefs, and certainly not enough to justify such a pervasive, industry-wide emphasis.

The editors speculate that group promoters and their donors focus on women because women, above men, can be collected into groups. Many social conventions in cultures across the world encourage females to be congenial, even compliant; when it comes to promoting the adoption of a new practice, women are prime targets. It is easier to gather obedient wives and daughters than to collar skeptical husbands and sons. But even this speculation is inconclusive. Again, we have no evidence.

We are seeing, at last, more development agencies making concerted efforts to include men and children. In Central America, Catholic Relief Services is finding that more men are joining groups once reserved for women or are starting their own groups. Plan International in West Africa recently included youth in its group promotion. In the Indian states of Andhra Pradesh and Karnataka, men's self-help groups are promoted as part of the nationwide effort to deal with the problem of small-farmer suicides.

## What We Should Conclude

### We may conclude that groups offer an alternative to microfinance institutions

In late 2006 one of our editors conducted interviews with two groups of women in Bangladesh, the world capital of traditional microfinance. Those interviewed were adamant that their groups served them better than any of the internationally renowned MFIs, or "banks," as the women called them, whose branches were within sight of where they were sitting. They were asked why.

They answered that the cost of loans from the big MFIs was too high, and much more important, when dealing with these institutions the women themselves did not keep the interest on borrowing; it went to the banks. The women also said that the bank employees were often rude; that group meetings were arranged according to the bank's convenience, not that of the members; and that the women preferred to take loans when they needed them, not when the bank's schedule demanded. The women also claimed that the banks were for better-off people; they spoke of the banks as a reader of this book might speak of a private wealth-management institution in Zurich or the Cayman Islands.

These women's reactions may have been unusual, but they are worth noting nonetheless. Their groups were part of a trial of the savings-group methodology undertaken by the Chars Livelihood Project (CLP) in Northern Bangladesh, and the results of the trial are thoroughly documented.[1] The trial promoted 849 groups, with about 18,000 members, between September 2006 and July 2008; 827 of these groups were still active in July 2008. About half of the abiding groups were in areas well served by MFIs, but the members voiced a clear preference for their own groups, for both saving and borrowing.

In some places and for some people, savings groups may offer better services than MFIs. Groups are often the only way that very poor people, who live in physically remote locales, have any access to savings services other than hiding savings in their mattresses. Likewise, people living in areas where institutions are insecure, or where services may vanish amid civil unrest, or where formal services may be denied for social reasons are probably best served by savings groups.

### We should conclude that groups are an institution

This book began by tracing the experience of traditional financial practices—"customary groups," which have taken hold in countries around the world. The number and influence of these groups continue to grow. Pradhan told the story of a *dhukuti* in Nepal, which coalesced into a full-fledged financial institution. Seibel described something similar occurring in Bali, but on a larger scale. "Saving, investing savings or loans to the benefit of the family, and repaying loans all positively affect one's *karma*," Seibel explained. "Wasting one's resources and failing to settle debts have a negative impact." Scarcity of formal financial resources, the utility of savings groups, and cultural imperatives combine in different ways to make powerful financial institutions. We predict the number of these "banks from the bottom" will continue to rise.

Not only will additional institutions surface from a tide of informal groups, they will bubble up from promoted groups as well. Indeed, many MFIs in India have evolved rather complex structures that began from the promotion of savings groups.

*We should conclude that groups are inventive*

Groups solve a host of problems on their own, with limited influence or assistance from the outside. One editor was told that in Niger groups mark their meetings with pebbles; each meeting occupies a particular position in a sequence of meetings, and a fresh pebble, added to other pebbles, denotes the number of meetings that remain until the group cashes out. Groups guard funds with different padlocks and keys, and they use their own system of oral recall to record what each member owes and what each has deposited.

When released from the prescription of experts, groups arrive at valuable, home-grown solutions. Cases from groups in Haiti, Mali, El Salvador, and India point to group creativity. In Haiti, one editor witnessed members of a group decide that each member should have a cow, the cow representing a good source of income. By hitching a special ROSCA to the savings group, each member was able to save up for her livestock purchase. In Mali, groups wanted to boost their respective savings funds; when groups clustered with other groups at larger meetings, they ran a ROSCA with different groups taking turns at receiving the full purse.

We expect to see sophisticated services emerge from older groups. We saw this in Sharma's and Matthews's description of the *xonchois xamitis* of Lower Assam. Some groups require members to make a single, initial deposit, similar to a fixed deposit at a bank, while others require members to make a series of deposits across a year or several years. Members are able to vary the ways in which their small streams of income pool into assets and then mature, in much the same way that participants of more formal financial systems diversify their investment portfolios.

*We may conclude that groups are resilient*

As champions of local wisdom, contributors to this book caution against excessive engineering of groups. Most argue for simplicity. "Less is more," our writers seem to say. And within this collection we have some confirmation that a sudden exit of promoters might actually strengthen the permanence of groups.

In both Odell's account of groups in Nepal, and Ahmed's and Ledgerwood's account of groups in Pakistan, we saw that the abrupt halt of assistance by promoters did not lead, as expected, to the dissolution of groups. In fact, the opposite happened. The majority of groups persisted for years, gathering in more members, further refining their procedures, and reassembling themselves as needed. In Nepal, groups weathered a national political crisis while impressively increasing their numbers. In Pakistan, groups unattended by promoters and scattered across isolated pockets of the Karakoram have remained intact for years.

## What We May Conclude Someday—Our Predictions

### We predict less "group casting" and more broadcasting

So far, most promoters stamp out groups according to a pre-cut pattern. Growth of groups is mechanical. A promoter might manufacture one group, which in turn forms two more, and so on, until all households within a perimeter are part of one group or another. While this approach to group production proves groups indeed can be made, the approach is inefficient and will not achieve the type of outreach that may be possible with modern forms of communication.

Inevitably, we believe government and private organizations will exploit more broadcast forms of group development. For example, radio programs might bring important messages and stories about savings. News and entertainment programs might accelerate the expansion of groups, and offer counsel on ways to improve savings and investment practices. Record-keeping and budgeting advice might be coupled with related themes such as addressing household crises, marketing farm produce, or managing the registry of property.

The use of other media could also boost the spread of groups and distribute important savings concepts to a wider audience. We expect to see more and better use of mobile-phone communications, television, and the Internet, or simpler messages conveyed by billboards, newspapers, and even advertising on buses and taxis.

This discussion of the spread of groups brings us to another prediction: we foresee increased networking among members. Today, groups are physically linked to one another by promoters, who act as gatekeepers of information and group assembly. Promoters decide when and how members of different groups will meet one another and under what circumstances. Communication is one dimensional: the promoter tells the group what to do. Promoter-led group information, often formulaic and unadjusted to local circumstance, restricts the collective advocacy of group members. Better technology, however, and multidirectional flows of information might encourage members to self-organize. We expect that broader use of such technology will nudge the sector away from its current emphasis on *promoter* agency toward an emphasis on *member* agency.

### We predict that groups will intensify their ability to attract additional social and financial services

Already formed and motivated to meet, and with collective funds to invest, savings groups draw in services related to health, agriculture, and education. They inspire the construction of new roads, schools, clinics, and irrigation networks. As groups congeal, new services congeal around them. Groups attract and will continue to attract programs that combat human trafficking, malaria, polio, and domestic violence. They motivate moneylenders to charge a fairer rate of interest, and bankers to extend credit for business use. They convince local police and courts to uphold laws, landlords to relinquish ill-gotten land, and factory managers to release child laborers. Groups have played a big part in pulling in new services and claiming rights, but so have governments, commercial actors, and NGOs. We see an upward trend of group-promoted justice, bolstered by the support of governments, NGOs, and other development agencies.

### We predict that groups are growing members of commercial value chains

Larger enterprises will continue to tap the infrastructure of savings groups to market their products and services. Hindustan

Lever Ltd. of India sells its salt packets[2] through savings-group members who are trained as dealers as well as promoters of health messages.[3] SELCO,[4] a producer of affordable lighting products, also in India, has included savings groups as an important element in marketing and finance chains. Members who sell and finance the SELCO products deem lighting investment a good one; it allows consumers to extend business hours, gives children light to read by, and reduces harmful use of kerosene. As commercial players continue to use groups to distribute or finance products and services, we expect negative consequences to accompany the positive ones, so we must all beware.

## Further Questions We Might Ask

Savings groups, arguably, are a defense against financial hardship. They are a platform onto which development agencies and businesses can fasten social and commercial services. They are a catalyst for the advocacy of human rights.

Yet we wonder whether encouraging their promotion is a wise or justifiable way to provide safer ways to save and cheaper ways to borrow, or whether savings groups replace more effective forms of community organizing and social justice. Have we become blinded?

Sadly, there are many millions of people who live in harsh conditions, and we have little reason to hope that their circumstances soon will change for the better. We, who read or write this book, are more fortunate, and we should hope and work for the day when everyone has access to the flexible and secure services that we ourselves enjoy. In the meantime, we should consider savings groups as a way to provide some measure of relief to millions of people so much less fortunate than we.

## Notes

[1] David Panetta, *Review of the VSLA Strategy of the CLP* (Bogra, Bangladesh: Chars Livelihood Project, 2008).

[2] C. K. Prahalad, *The Fortune at the Bottom of the Pyramid: Eradicating Poverty through Profits* (Philadelphia, PA: Wharton School Publishing, 2006).

[3] P. Sharath Chandra Rao, Jeffrey B. Miller, Young Doo Wang, and John B. Byrne, "Energy-microfinance Intervention for below Poverty Line Households in India," *Energy Policy* 37, no. 5 (2009): 1694–1712.
[4] Ibid.

# Contributors

***Wajiha Ahmed*** earned a master's degree in development studies from the Fletcher School of Law and Diplomacy at Tufts University. Most recently, she worked for the Kashf Foundation's microfinance team in Lahore, Pakistan.

***Hugh Allen*** has worked in development since 1970, focusing for most of the last fifteen years on community-managed microfinance. In 2006, he founded VSL Associates to promote this approach through numerous multi-sectoral development agencies and southern NGOs. Among other publications, he has authored a program guide for setting up Village Savings and Loan Associations and has contributed to Practical Action's *What's Wrong with Microfinance?*

***Jeffrey Ashe*** is the director of community finance at Oxfam America and is responsible for the Saving for Change program. Prior to coming to Oxfam, Ashe founded Working Capital and served as its executive director. Ashe has published extensively in the microenterprise field and is the author of several books and articles on the topic. He holds a B.A. in political science from the University of California, Berkeley, and an M.A. in sociology from Boston University.

***Gaye Burpee***, Ph.D., works for Catholic Relief Services as the deputy regional director for Latin America and the Caribbean. She has served as director of the Technical Services Unit at CRS and as senior technical advisor for agriculture, covering Africa, Asia, and Latin America. Previously she worked for the International Center for Tropical Agriculture, the University of Michigan's Institute for Social Research, and as a Peace Corps volunteer in the West Indies.

***Eloisa Devietti*** is program assistant for the Community Finance Department at Oxfam America. At Oxfam she has been involved in projects to facilitate regional office and headquarters coordination and has most recently conducted this assessment of the Saving for Change microfinance groups in El Salvador. She holds a master's degree in international relations from Boston University.

***Matthew Griffith*** is an independent consultant focusing on community finance and livelihoods. He has worked with marginalized communities in Russia, the United States, and Ethiopia. Most recently, he worked with the Feinstein International Center at Tufts University on a project focusing on the financial resilience of disaster-affected populations. He received a master's degree from the Fletcher School of Law and Diplomacy.

***Mabel Guevara***, who has a B.A. in business administration from the University of El Salvador, began working with Catholic Relief Services El Salvador in 2005 and became coordinator for the savings-led microfinance initiative in 2008. In this role she coordinates training and provides capacity building and technical assistance to local partners and promoters. Under her leadership the initiative has grown to include fifty-three savings groups in the poorest regions of rural El Salvador.

***Malcolm Harper*** is the chairman of M-CRIL. He was the chairman of BASIX of Hyderabad for ten years and was the founding editor of *Small Enterprise Development* (now *Enterprise Development and Microfinance*). He has worked on poverty issues in South Asia, East Asia, Africa, Latin America and the Caribbean, the Middle East and Gulf area, and the United Kingdom. Harper was educated at Oxford, Harvard, and Nairobi.

***Kristin Helmore*** has covered development issues for more than twenty years, reporting from Africa, Asia, and Latin America. Her work has included ground-breaking coverage of microfinance in Bangladesh, India, and Africa. Her articles in the *Christian Science Monitor* received numerous awards, including the Overseas Press Club Award, the Sigma Delta Chi Award in Journalism, the Population Institute's Global Media Award, and the President's End Hunger Award.

***Elke Jahns*** is a Ph.D. student at the Fletcher School with an interest in rural poverty and resilience. She has worked with women's groups in Tanzania, Kenya, and Chile, in addition to a variety of projects in sustainable agriculture, environmental education, women's rights, and HIV/AIDS prevention and support. Most recently, she studied the impact of climate change on the rural poor in Central America.

***Yang Saing Koma*** is president of CEDAC, a Cambodian NGO promoting family-based ecological agriculture and participatory development, conducting research, and offering training, publication, and marketing support. Koma has been a lecturer in farming-system research, development, and management at both the Royal University of Agriculture and International University.

***Joanna Ledgerwood*** joined the Aga Khan Foundation in 2007. Prior to moving to Geneva, Ledgerwood worked on microfinance issues in Uganda, the Philippines, and elsewhere in Africa, Asia, and Latin America. She is a frequent presenter at international conferences and has written numerous papers and books, including *Transforming MFIs* with Victoria White (2006) and the *Microfinance Handbook* (1998), both published by the World Bank.

***Brett Hudson Matthews*** is managing partner of Mathwood Consulting Company. The mission of Mathwood Consulting Company is to help the world's poorest billion rural people gain access to community-based microfinance.

***Janina Matuszeski*** is research coordinator for Oxfam America's Community Finance Department. She oversees the operational, qualitative, and quantitative research for the Saving for Change program in Mali, Cambodia, and El Salvador. She was a Peace Corps volunteer in Mali for two years. Matuszeski has a Ph.D. in economics from Harvard University.

***Anthony Murathi*** has worked in microfinance and development sectors for a decade and a half. He now works for CARE International in Kenya managing a group savings and loan project covering nine districts in West Kenya. He believes that grassroots microfinance is the "way to go" in mitigating the effects of the global financial crisis in Africa.

*Marcia Odell* is the director of WORTH, which has reached nearly 200,000 women in Asia and Africa. Since heading up the pilot program in Nepal, she has helped launch WORTH programs in Kenya, Cambodia, Tanzania, Zambia, Congo (DRC), Ethiopia, and Uganda. She has an M.B.A. from the Whittemore School of Business and Economics (UNH), an M.S. from Wheelock College, and a B.A. and Ph.D. from Cornell University.

*Nelly Otieno* has worked in microcredit for nineteen years in Kenya, promoting savings and credit cooperatives, Grameen model institutions and the revolving loan funds. She introduced the VSLA methodology in Kenya in 2004 and works on the improvement of community managed micro credit in Kenya.

*Vinod Parmeshwar*, community finance manager at Oxfam America, is responsible for overall program management of Oxfam America's Saving for Change program. Parmeshwar is an expert in adult learning pedagogy. He is an adjunct faculty member at Brandeis University in the United States and has Southern New Hampshire University's Microenterprise Development Certificate in Africa. He holds a master's degree in business administration from the Indian Institute of Management–Calcutta.

*Shailee Pradhan* is a dual-degree student at the Fletcher School of Law and Diplomacy, and the Friedman School of Nutrition Science and Policy at Tufts University. A native of Nepal, she first learned of microfinance through her mother, Meenu Pradhan, who familiarized her with the concept of savings and credit. Since then, she has conducted field research for microfinance institutions in Bangladesh and Malawi.

*Paul Rippey* worked in microcredit in Africa for two decades and now devotes his time to promoting savings groups in Africa and Asia. He also works to promote solar lamps and biomass briquettes for people in remote areas, and he argues that savings groups are a natural and inevitable marketing channel for clean energy products.

*Bridget Bucardo Rivera* received her master's degree in international political economy and development from Fordham University in 2009. She recently completed an internship with

Catholic Relief Services El Salvador, where she worked in the Livelihoods Department. She is currently working as an international development fellow with CRS Nicaragua.

***Hans Dieter Seibel*** is a professor emeritus at Cologne University, a senior fellow at the Development Research Center (ZEF) of the University of Bonn, and vice-chairman of the Consultative Committee of the Common Fund for Commodities. He specializes in development and microfinance, self-help groups as financial intermediaries, self-help group-bank linkages, and agricultural development bank reform.

***Abhijit Sharma*** is an assistant professor at the Indian Institute of Bank Management, Guwahati. His interests are in financial markets in remote and sparsely populated regions, particularly community-based financial institutions. He frequently serves as a consultant for banks, microfinance institutions, the government, and the central bank regarding issues of financial inclusion.

***Girija Srinivasan***, consultant in development and microfinance, has worked in the sector for twenty-five years. She has broad experience with the major donors, NGOs, and microfinance institutions in India and has consulted internationally in Bangladesh, Vietnam, Sri Lanka, and the Netherlands. She has also written books and several articles on microfinance.

***N. Srinivasan*** is a consultant in development, rural, and microfinance with strong interests in development finance and development economics. Srinivasan worked with National Bank for Agriculture and Rural Development for twenty-four years. He authored the "State of the Sector Report on Microfinance in India, 2008." Currently, he is an independent consultant to a large range of donors, governments, and practitioner consortia in both India and Vietnam.

***Guy Vanmeenen***, Catholic Relief Services' senior technical advisor for microfinance in Africa, developed the organization's savings-led microfinance strategy, the Savings and Internal Lending Communities (SILC) model, and supported its roll out in more than twenty-five African countries. Vanmeenen has fifteen years of microfinance experience.

**Kim Wilson** is a lecturer at the Fletcher School, where she teaches microfinance, development, and inclusive markets. Previously, she was with Catholic Relief Services as a senior advisor in microfinance. Prior to her work in international development, she was a principal of a Boston-based merchant bank that focused on franchising.

**Julie Zollmann** is a master's degree student at the Fletcher School of Law and Diplomacy, where she is studying inclusive markets from economic and business perspectives. Prior to Fletcher, Zollmann worked with CARE for two years helping design and manage foundation-funded grants for emergency relief, agriculture, value chains, and savings groups. She also served as an HIV outreach Peace Corps volunteer in rural Swaziland.

# Index

# Also from Kumarian Press...

## Microfinance:

**Freedom From Want:** The Remarkable Success Story of BRAC, the Global Grassroots Organization that's Winning the Fight Against Poverty
Ian Smillie

**The Poor Always Pay Back:** The Grameen II Story
Asif Dowla and Dipal Barua

**The Commercialization of Microfinance:** Balancing Business and Development
Edited by Deborah Drake and Elisabeth Rhyne

**Savings Services for the Poor:** An Operational Guide
Edited by Madeline Hirschland

## New and Forthcoming:

**Just Give Money to the Poor:** The Development Revolution from the Global South
Joseph Hanlon, Armando Barrientos and David Hulme

**Confronting Microfinance:** Undermining Sustainable Development
Edited by Milford Bateman

**Extreme Microfinance:** Savings Groups on the Financial Frontier
Kim Wilson

**Artisans and Fair Trade:** Crafting Development
Mary Littrell and Marsha Dickson

Visit Kumarian Press at **www.kpbooks.com** or call **toll-free 800.232.0223** for a complete catalog.

*Kumarian Press, located in Sterling, Virginia, is a forward-looking, scholarly press that promotes active international engagement and an awareness of global connectedness.*